a R🔵ADMAP

to Modern Slavery Compliance and a Sustainable Supply Chain

THE POWER TO BRING CHANGE, MANAGE RISK,
IMPROVE ESG SCORES AND UNLOCK VALUE

CARSTEN PRIMDAL

TESTIMONIALS

'With this book, Carsten has provided a clear, practical pathway to identifying and solving these important problems in the supply chain. From an investment perspective, taking the steps outlined contributes to effective risk management, improved resilience, and ultimately continuity. Anyone serious about securing their supply chain should heed the advice given in this book.'

Timothy King CFA, CIO, Melior Investment Management

'In this important work, Carsten Primdal shares the lessons learnt over many years of personal experience, making this book compelling reading for any company that is serious about investigating the possibility of forced labour within their supply chains and provides guidance on the most appropriate remedial action. We are presented with an excellent overview of this complex domain and provided with practical guidelines and templates to aid with internal compliance and with meeting external legislative obligations.'

Dr David Cooke, Konica Minolta Business Solutions Australia

'This book is an excellent, easy-to-read guide with practical steps on how to take action when you suspect unsatisfactory activities in the supply chain. Based on his personal experience, Carsten identifies the early warning signs and what to look for when embarking on the essential journey towards ethical sourcing and a sustainable supply chain. In his book, Carsten breaks complex and difficult risk-management processes into simple and operational steps, supported by useful questionnaires and checklists to support you on the way.'

Irene Sobotta, Research, Development and Adoption Program Manager Integrity Systems Company

'Modern slavery has become the primary ESG issue of our times – driven by NGO, media, intergovernmental and investor focus and action, and more recently regulation across multiple jurisdictions. However, managing these risks effectively is far from a simple exercise. Carsten presents an accessible and practical guide to identifying, managing and remedying labour risks in a supply chain, based on direct hands-on experience from the procurement team right back to the factory level in source countries.'

Matt Willson, Associate Director, Sustainability, Westpac Institutional Bank

'Companies affect human rights (including the challenge of modern slavery) every day in their interactions with employees, suppliers, consumers, partners and communities. Carsten's insightful and practical approach in this book addresses a company's responsibility to respect human rights both within its own operations, including joint ventures and other forms of partnerships, and in its business relationships with public and private entities in its value chain, including suppliers, labour contractors, distributors and business customers.'

Andrew Petersen, CEO, Business Council for Sustainable Development Australia

WITH GRATITUDE

I feel privileged to have had the opportunity to write this, my second book.

When I started out writing my first book, *Red Flag: Your guide to risk management when buying in China*, four years ago, I had no idea where that would take me, and that one day I would be the author of two books, and with plans for many other books – yet to be written.

But to actually get these words to paper, I must first of all thank my family.

Thank you to my wife, Jie, and to my three boys, Marc, Max and Matt, who all have provided crucial support and encouragement, enabling me to write this book.

Thank you to my mother, and my sister and her amazing family in Denmark, my parents in law and my sister in law and her family in China.

Thank you to my friends, contacts and clients, many of whom have helped with inspiration, feedback and suggestions.

Finally, a big thank you to my editor Michael Hanrahan and the team at Michael Hanrahan Publishing, for their support and professionalism in turning the draft manuscript into a real book.

Project management and text design by Michael Hanrahan Publishing
Cover design by Peter Reardon

Disclaimer
The material in this publication is of the nature of general comment only, and does not represent professional advice. It is not intended to provide specific guidance for particular circumstances and it should not be relied on as the basis for any decision to take action or not take action on any matter which it covers. Readers should obtain professional advice where appropriate, before making any such decision. To the maximum extent permitted by law, the author and publisher disclaim all responsibility and liability to any person, arising directly or indirectly from any person taking or not taking action based on the information in this publication.

CONTENTS

RECOMMENDED READING

If you would like to gain an insight into a real slave's experiences, Vannak Prum's book *The Dead Eye and the Deep Blue Sea: A graphic memoir of modern slavery* is a real eye-opener. Vannak is a survivor of slavery on a fishing vessel in Thailand, where he was deceived into leaving his home country, Cambodia, by a recruitment agent to support his wife and unborn baby. The job in Thailand turned out to be anything but what was promised, and instead he was held as a slave on a fishing vessel in the Gulf of Thailand, only to escape at the Malaysian coastline, being picked up by police and then sold once again to a rubber plantation.

The book is a revelation – and not of the pleasant kind. Vannak is an amazing artist, and most of the book is in fact his drawings of his experiences. This makes for some extremely graphic and violent imagery of what happened to the slaves on the vessels. It is highly recommended, although not as a bedtime story!

FOREWORD

With increased regulatory focus on labour rights in supply chains and with increased investor interest in this area, I welcome *A Roadmap to Modern Slavery Compliance and a Sustainable Supply Chain* as a useful and hands-on guide for companies to enhance their ethical sourcing practices.

The responsible investment industry is a fast-growing area, and while historically the main focus has been on environmental issues, there is growing investor interest in social issues. Increasingly, investors understand the links between sustainable supply chains and sustainable earnings.

At the heart of it, if a company's business model relies on underpaid workers, weak regulation, poor enforcement of labour laws or even illegal activities, such as slavery, current earnings will unlikely be sustainable over time. Also, the way a company deals with its suppliers can act as a proxy for management quality.

The UN Sustainable Development Goals and the Australian *Modern Slavery Act* as well as other regulatory developments in other jurisdictions will likely drive further investor focus on these issues.

Supply chains are becoming increasingly complex and global, which means practical guides, such as this book, will become ever more important for companies to navigate the issues.

Måns Carlsson-Sweeny
Head of ESG Research, Ausbil Investment Management Limited

INTRODUCTION: DISCOVERING WHAT'S REALLY GOING ON

'WE WON'T EXPORT THESE TO EUROPE'

My personal journey in this area started in 2001, when I was working at an automotive engineering company near Barcelona, Spain.

I was the Area Manager, responsible for developing sales to Asian economies, and the area of focus for initial market penetration was to sell homologation services to Asian companies wishing to acquire documentation that would allow them to sell their products into Europe. To meet this need, homologation is a requirement, establishing that a product meets the legal requirements that make the product safe to be used on the road.

On one of my trips to India, I visited an Indian brake pad factory, with a strong desire to start exporting their product to Europe.

Arriving onsite in the early hours, we started out with a nice meeting in a comfortable and airconditioned meeting room in the management building, being served tea, some sweets, and chatting with the Managing Director. He then suggested we take a tour of the facility, to show off their – as they like to call things in India – 'world-class facilities'.

The MD delegated to a team member to give us the 'grand tour', and left us.

Walking through the facility, we came to a production hall, probably around 10 × 15 meters and with around 100 workstations, all occupied with male workers hunched down over their work.

While the hall was large, it had minimal light, and it was dull and dusty. On closer inspection, I could see that the dust looked like soot. Each worker held a brake pad and was grinding off the rough edges stemming from the moulding and baking process. This is what produced the dark soot covering every surface in the room.

I asked the manager showing us the facilities: 'What material are you using?'

He replied: 'Asbestos ... '

I was stunned. I didn't know what to say.

And then he continued: '... but don't worry – we won't export these to Europe. In Europe it can't contain asbestos, so we will not use it.'

His only concern was about the material composition of the brake pads and ensuring that they would be compliant with European regulations.

I wanted to leave immediately.

But what about the workers? The workers with no choice, no options?

No-one deserves to be worked to death. And on top of this, these men were probably so poorly educated that they had no idea of the degree of danger they put themselves in doing a job that barely paid the bills, and most certainly would not provide any discretionary income to support their families if (when?) they were hit by disease. Today, in 2019, I wonder how many of these people are still alive, and – sadly – my guess is it's not that many.

On a personal note, it so happened that my own father, about one year later, was diagnosed with Mesothelioma, a cancer caused by asbestos fibres – and he had never worked with asbestos. In fact, he was a partner at PwC in Denmark, and wasn't exposed other than from living and working in buildings with asbestos in the walls and ceilings, and perhaps from occasionally inhaling asbestos fibres released by cars in the street.

This only doubled my level of concern for the workers: if you can't even be safe from asbestos when you *don't* work with it, why do we expect anyone to endure those kinds of working conditions?

This experience in India stuck with me for a long time, and made me want to do something about this terrible situation. This is why I decided to educate myself as an SA8000 auditor[1], in late 2007. That training became the starting point to another chapter in my career, because soon after I completed that training I was approached to project manage a large project in China which had a sister project in Bangladesh. The project was contracted through the German development organisation GTZ[2] (now GIZ), for a major German retailer.

This set me on a course to get on-the-ground experience in China, Bangladesh and Cambodia, and not just the typical fly-in–fly-out experience most people in supply chain management get when dealing with China. In China alone, I worked with (and attended production sites of) over 300 factories across Guangdong, Fujian, Zhejiang, Jiangsu, Shanghai, Shandong and Beijing. We undertook to deliver capacity-building projects on behalf of mostly European retailers, which consisted of:

- site visits
- managing Corrective Action Plans and Improvement Plans
- delivering lectures and workshops to factory management
- delivering training to workers while onsite
- establishing base information so we could assess progress.

---

1   SA8000 is a social compliance standard, widely considered the best in class. An SA8000 auditor audits factory working conditions and management systems, using a range of skills and data-gathering methods, including site inspections, worker interviews, and document and policy reviews. A skilled auditor will use triangulation to call out issues which are not entirely as they appear to be at first sight.

2   GTZ/GIZ is the German equivalent of Ausaid (now called 'Australia Aid') and USAID.

Later I was approached to assist BSCI with delivering training on behalf of their members to their producers in China and Cambodia.[3]

During this time, we delivered on average one five-day workshop every month, with an audience of 250 to 300 people each day. We reached over 2,500 producers in China and Cambodia with our training.

I personally experienced finding and remediating child labour, document retention issues, delayed and reduced payments, workers in perilous situations due to the excessive recruitment fees paid to recruitment agents, and many, many more problems that put workers' health, safety and wellbeing in jeopardy. I have taken part in remediating cases of slavery-like conditions, and setting up mitigating systems to prevent future incidents.

I have no need to wordsmith stories and I don't have a background in corporate communications fine-tuning other people's stories. I also don't claim to have coined any phrases I didn't coin, nor do I adorn myself with borrowed feathers from second-hand experiences.

I have no need for any of that, because my experience is real and firsthand, and I was the person responsible for solving these issues.

This is the experience I am sharing with you in this book, so that you can understand these issues and how to deal with them.

CORPORATE SOCIAL RESPONSIBILITY SHOULD NOT BE OPTIONAL

'All human beings are born free and equal in dignity and rights. They are endowed with reason and conscience and should act towards one another in a spirit of brotherhood.'

United Nations Universal Declaration of Human Rights

---

3   BSCI is a business initiative aimed at pooling resources to improve working conditions at supplier sites deep in the supply chain. BSCI stands for 'Business Social Compliance Initiative'. 'Amfori' is their new name, since 2018.

Many large businesses consider corporate social responsibility (CSR), business ethics and sustainability a cost that they can choose to take on board or chose to disregard.

Why is that?

Are we not all obliged to behave well and treat each other ethically?

Imagine for a moment that a car company said, 'It's too complex to comply with safety regulations and consumer expectations, so we are going to take the calculated risk of not doing so'.

Would anyone accept such a company? Would it have a market for long?

Or how about a company deciding not to complete their annual report, with the excuse that: 'There is too much information to be able to reach a reliable conclusion on the status of the business, so we chose to leave out any information where we are not certain'?

If it's not okay to ignore product safety rules or reporting compliance requirements, why is it okay for a company to not know where their products are sourced, and under what conditions they are made?

Yes, it can be complicated and cumbersome to provide transparency, but what is the alternative?

If you are with me so far, let's get started …

Many people call the path to sustainability a 'journey'. But a journey implies a process without fixed way points, and to a degree perhaps not even a fixed end point.

Imagine for a moment that a CEO described a company as being 'on a journey to profit'. While that may be appropriate in a turnaround situation, it is certainly not appropriate in the normal running of a business, where any activity should support either today's or tomorrow's profits.

The same applies to sustainability. It is not a journey but an investment in tomorrow. It helps to improve the lives of millions of people, and provides opportunities and mitigates risks for businesses, all while supporting the business into the future. As such, it shouldn't be a 'journey' but a plan, with established milestones and deliverables.

This book was written with the intention to help you establish the way points and set up a framework to define deliverables. The benefit will be a level playing field for all operators. Ideally the system would be arranged in such a way that if businesses cannot prove that their products are sourced in sustainable and ethical ways, they are simply not allowed to sell them. So, let's get sanctions, confiscation of profits, suspension of business licences, and other measures in place.

Those who play by the rules will benefit, and those who don't will suffer the consequences.

Apart from the legal compliance aspect, I, personally, think this is about good business, about being honest, and doing the right thing for both workers and consumers, without taking short cuts. Businesses will be stronger for it, and the ones that take short cuts to gain a temporary advantage will be penalised eventually, either through reduced sales and profits or by being closed down by legal action.

This may seem harsh, but if all play by the same rules, that doesn't matter.

Finally, it is not 'only' about slavery. Slavery is reprehensible, without a doubt. You can't eliminate it though if you don't look at other aspects of unethical and criminal behaviour. So, you must remember to focus on more than just slavery, and address the system that produced it.

Businesses' adherence to sustainable and ethical business practices can open doors, when required. It never closes doors when it does not matter, but it will close doors if not good enough when it does matter. And its absence will never open any doors.

From a purely business perspective, the key question is if saving a bit of cash is really worth the risk in the long term, and if you lose out on opportunities as a result of taking a short position on sustainability which didn't pan out as expected.

Despite recent international developments trying to halt and even reverse the last 30 years of globalisation, the global economy is hugely dependent on international trade. This international trade has come with advantages as well as disadvantages. Consumers are now starting to demand that some of these disadvantages are addressed.

One such issue is the conditions under which products being offered for sale domestically are manufactured in overseas supply chains. Not only are consumers concerned about the often appalling working conditions in these far-away factories, they are also uneasy about job losses at home due to overseas low-wage competition, product quality, and a range of other issues. Businesses are also concerned with what may appear to be unfair practices, when some companies make use of a non-compliant workforce, substandard materials and illegal methods to gain a competitive advantage for their products.

But what is a competitive disadvantage in one instance can be turned upside-down and become a positive diversifier, if applied correctly. One such diversifying advantage lies in adopting ethical and sustainable standards that respect the rights and concerns of humans and the environment.

Legislators intend for large corporates to be the drivers of change. If you are a supplier to a large corporate where reporting is a compliance requirement, expect to be asked to feed in your information to support your client's reporting requirements.

WHO IS THIS BOOK FOR?

With the introduction of a *Modern Slavery Act* on both Commonwealth and a State level in NSW, there is a fair bit of anxiety among the people who are obliged to implement this new legislation in their business practices. I am guessing this is because the task ahead can seem daunting, to say the least. However, like anything else, a task parsed into manageable-sized chunks is more achievable.

To help with parsing the task, I wrote this book to share my experience in running this type of project. This book is for anyone who hasn't run a sustainable supply chain project in an at-risk country, and who has little or no idea where to start.

While this is not rocket science, I spent plenty of time making mistakes, and there is no need for others to repeat these. That is why I decided to put my experiences in writing, for you to benefit from.

So, this book is not written for the sustainability professional who is already dealing with these issues, although many sustainability professionals come from a background in human rights law or corporate communication, and have never been to China or Bangladesh for more than seven or eight days in one trip. If that is the case, readers with little onsite experience can benefit from reading this book the same way I can benefit from the legal perspective shared by a human rights lawyer (which I am not).

This book is intended to help reduce the level of misperception around what should and must be done, how teams new to this field can approach the program of work, and how it can be itemised and partitioned beneficially to all parties, obtaining maximum benefit for the minimum required effort – and without repeating the mistakes already made by others.

In particular, this book has been written to inform Heads of Procurement, Heads of Supply Chain, Heads of Communications, Heads of Corporate/Legal Counsel, as well as the C-suite, allowing them an understanding that will simplify the process, provide a critical level of internal understanding, and minimise the risk of being gullible in regards to external consultants who would like to provide the gold-plated solution, have next to nothing to sell, or who are overpricing their services and delivering with inexperienced staff.

1. WHAT IS AN ETHICAL SUPPLY CHAIN?

While corporate responsibility covers areas such as social, environmental and ethical business conduct and compliance, in general terms:

- 'social' refers to labour conditions, such as slavery or child labour

- 'environmental' refers to resource usage and pollution

- 'ethical' refers to bribery, corruption and fraud.

These specific definitions are quite technical, and are even unpractical because the problems they are used to describe often are part of a constellation of overlapping issues. In addition, everyone has their own definitions of what each term covers, making it ambiguous and very difficult to address. For these reasons, these terms are used interchangeably throughout this book and should be understood according to the context in which they appear.

SocialCompliance SustainableSupplyChain SustainableBusiness EthicalBehaviour CR CSR EthicalBusiness CorporateSocialResponsibility CorporateResponsibility ResponsibleBusiness EthicalSupplyChain

THE TWO REALITIES DRIVING THE NEED FOR SUSTAINABILITY

Two mutually reinforcing drivers underpin the need to enhance the movement away from unethical, socially and environmentally exploitative business practices:

1. Repelling customers: Such practices are often criminal, and overexploit both human and natural resources. Engaging in criminal conduct can result in criminal charges being laid and the business must apply resources defending itself. In the process, consumers can lose trust and walk away. If such practices become public knowledge, customers may be repelled from buying.

2. Attracting customers: Consumers are becoming more conscious of their personal impact on the world and want to minimise this by purchasing from likeminded companies. This presents an opportunity for businesses ready to act and who walk the talk. This is an opportunity to attract and retain customers.

While compliance with the law is a given in most businesses, what happens in the supply chain is often seen as 'outside our control'. Consumer sentiment can sometimes be difficult to gauge, but what is certain is that more and more consumers have an expectation that businesses understand what is going on in what was traditionally regarded as outside the direct control of the business.

Studies show that consumers are looking for companies whose products have minimal, if any, negative impacts on society:

According to surveys done in the US:

- 40% of consumers are interested in ethically or sustainably sourced products

- 32% of consumers check product labels for claims about sustainability

- 25% of consumers actively look for product origins when making a purchase decision.

For businesses, the key is if consumers are willing to pay extra for ethically sourced items:

- 52% would pay more for food and beverage products if they are ethically sourced

- 45% would pay more for clothing and footwear

- 44% would pay more for pharmaceuticals.

And how much extra would they pay?

- 30% of US consumers would pay 5% more for a product that is ethically sourced

- 28% would pay up to 20% more.

Source: Spend Matters

Similar numbers can be expected in Australia. This makes a compelling business case not just to remain compliant and stay out of trouble but also from a monetary perspective.

However, to make an informed decision on how deep to go, it's important to understand what the issues are and where, why and how they occur, along with the drivers in key markets. Is this simply a nice vision based on an idealistic world view *or* is it a regulatory nightmare *or* the next big opportunity? Or perhaps a bit of all three?

In any case, there is a need to act on this increasingly important issue for consumers.

AN OFFICE SUPPLIES COMPANY

While being a well-known and large office supplies company, only few realise that this company has a very decent-size sustainability team, and require most of their suppliers to be able to demonstrate what they do to advance sustainability. This is in the company's procurement policy and, surprising to many, it is not just a document but actually something they apply stringently.

To ensure compliance, suppliers are required to become members of SEDEX, and provide audit details, as well as engage with the company to constantly improve.

So, if you want to be a supplier to this business, that's another requirement to fulfil, and don't be surprised if your claims are looked into.

Like any other business that is serious about sustainability, this supplier of office equipment needs to be able to demonstrate that their suppliers are as serious about their commitments as they are themselves and that they take safeguarding of their customers' reputations seriously.

2. UNETHICAL ACTIVITIES WITHIN SUPPLY CHAINS

Even with today's heavy emphasis on corporate 'risk management', every supply chain contains inherent risks that have the potential to derail its activities and close down its participants. Some risks are location-based – such as earthquakes, floods, and fires – and are impossible to predict. At best, they are mitigated by insurance. Human-generated hazards, on the other hand, are often predictable, detectable and preventable – assuming that business leadership wants to make the effort to mitigate the identified risks.

Identifying unethical or illegal activities within any supply chain can be challenging, however. Some unsavoury activities can be non-compliant or illegal in one jurisdiction but not in another, which confounds the capacity to discover and mitigate them with consistency.

THE THREE COMMON SUSTAINABLE SUPPLY CHAIN CHALLENGES

There are three overarching categories of unethical activities that can pop up at any juncture within any supply chain, regardless of its location:

- social exploitation

- resource exploitation

- ethical misconduct.

PrecariousEmployment
OccupationalHealth&Safety
Pollution
Fraud
BondedLabour
FairRemuneration
ResourceWastage
Effluent
Blackmail
Corruption
Bribery
MoneyLaundering
Discrimination
Emissions
Embezzlement
ChildLabour
Waste
Extortion
ProductLifecycle
FreedomofAssociation
DecentWorkingHours
EnvironmentalProtection
SpecialProtectionforYoungWorkers
EthicalBusinessBehaviour

SOCIAL EXPLOITATION

There are a number of issues related to social exploitation, such as paying less than minimum wages, demanding excess overtime without compensation, and child labour. Slavery is in the worst of categories, along with child labour. Slavery is defined as people being forced or sold to marry, provide sexual services, or for uncompensated labour. Slavery sparks vivid mental pictures of shackled slaves on slave boats crossing the Atlantic in the 17th century. As appalling as that trade was, modern slavery is every bit as bad – it's just less visible to the untrained eye. The Global Slavery Index recorded over 40 million people in modern slavery in 2016, which may even be a significant underrepresentation of the actual number. Antislavery.org reports an estimated 10 million children involved in global slavery, while another 151 million – 114 million of them under 14 years – are forced to work rather than go to school.

RESOURCE EXPLOITATION

Many suppliers are chosen because of their ability to deliver a decent product for a lower unit price. What is less obvious is often these producers are located in countries with a lax or nonexistent application of environmental laws and regulations, leading to environmental degradation and pollution of the local area. This often contributes to their low costs.

In some cases, they use their access to exploit resources as they fulfil their contractual obligations to overseas buyers; for example, many people have heard about so-called 'conflict minerals' or 'blood diamonds', where mining practices are unduly harsh on workers, local populations and the surrounding environment. But other mineral supply chains that gain less public notoriety – such as those that produce tin, talc or marble – are also are often fraught with illegal activities.

ETHICAL MISCONDUCT

Ethical misconduct takes many forms, including corruption, bribery, kickbacks, money laundering, embezzlement, blackmail, and extortion, to name just a few. In a supply chain setting, ethical misconduct occurs frequently and can be almost unnoticeable. Another dubious practice could be a part supplier in cahoots with a warehouse covertly substituting some parts for inferior products while splitting the difference in cost. While the swap may appear inconsequential, substandard parts could cause any number of problems to the company and its brand, and at the very least it highlights that the chain of custody is broken.

A MULTINATIONAL ELECTRONICS COMPANY

Being the sales and marketing arm of a large Japanese multinational in the document and information management industry, you might be inclined to think that this Australian sales arm does not need to consider its supply chain, and in particular whether it's sustainable or not.

However, dig a bit deeper and it is apparent that they are in fact a major buyer and reseller of paper, and a major user of transport. Having several sites across Australia and New Zealand, they also employ many people in cleaning and maintenance – which is notorious for exploitative labour practices.

While the manufacturing is done by the Japanese mother company, and they are members of the Responsible Business Alliance (formerly the Electronic Industry Citizenship Coalition), there are plenty of domestic issues to look into in Australia.

Further, several large customers were starting to mandate an increasing level of sustainability documentation as a condition of a continued business relationship.

To mitigate the risk, this business developed a five-step roadmap to a sustainable supply chain, and published the commitment publicly.

THE CONSEQUENCES

These three are often intertwined and/or happening in parallel with each other. Ultimately, every participant in every supply chain is at risk of paying the penalty for the unethical or unsustainable actions of another participant.

When viewed from the consumer's perspective – and acknowledging that consumers are the ultimate referee of corporate success – most shoppers aren't concerned about where within a supply chain the process has failed. They will walk away when they find out about problems, and in doing so hold all product contributors responsible, ultimately leaving them out of pocket.

And, because of the importance of supply chains in today's global economy, even small oversights can have large impacts on a business in the form of consumer boycotts, product recalls, strained or lost business partnerships, or even lawsuits as a result of incomplete and/or misleading statements; for example, if some information has been misrepresented in a corporate modern slavery statement.

Despite these realities, however, many companies continue to avoid the costs and attention needed to eradicate these practices from their production lines. By turning a deaf ear to this, businesses not only expose themselves to risk, they also leave money on the table.

In a 2017 Forbes survey of 800 supply chain executives, almost 80% of respondents asserted that their supply chains were 'responsible'; however, further investigation revealed that only 23% were specifically addressing climate change issues and 22% were specifically looking at child labour issues.

The research indicated that there remains a wide range of definitions for what it means to be 'responsible':

- Some of the companies had hired contractors to facilitate their ethical activities without doing more to ensure that those activities were in fact occurring.

- Others believed that having supply chain partners sign their code of conduct was sufficient action on their part to ensure that unethical activities would not happen.

- Still others had enforced labour and pay regulations but hadn't investigated the possibilities of environmental damage or corruption within their own organisations.

Businesses risk more than just scarring of their brands for going along with inappropriate elements within their supply architecture when they should have known better. Regulators can and will determine significant penalties for unethical business practices, which often escalate in direct relation to the harm they cause. In addition to penalties imposed, companies may also be made to absorb costs incurred for legal fees and court and litigation costs, along with potential damages from loss of consumer confidence.

3. DOMESTIC AND INTERNATIONAL RESPONSES TO SUSTAINABLE SUPPLY CHAIN ISSUES

Some countries are more focused on unethical business conduct than others. The sustainable supply chain has been a hot topic in the US and Europe for quite some time, which is also reflected in the actions taken.

> While slavery is abhorrent, you cannot separate it from other types of unethical behaviour. These problems often go hand in hand, and a supply chain utilising slaves as a source of labour is potentially just as prone to child labour and other violations. They will also have an extreme risk of being involved in money laundering, bribery and other types of ethical misconduct. As such, producing a modern slavery statement without addressing non-slavery issues is simply not meaningful.

To understand the international environment Australia is operating in, it's necessary to see where this issue is taken more seriously. Interestingly, countries taking more action (the top 10) to mitigate unethical practices are all located in Europe or North America. Conversely, the bottom 10 are almost all African nations.

Level of action to mitigate unethical practices

More action	Less action
Netherlands	North Korea
United States	Libya
United Kingdom	Eritrea
Sweden	Central African Republic
Belgium	Iran
Croatia	Equatorial Guinea
Spain	Burundi
Norway	Republic of Congo
Portugal	Sudan
Montenegro	Mauritania

Source: Global Slavery Index

It is also noteworthy that the top 10 are all affluent countries with a high degree of consumer choice.

Depending on which markets you intend to serve, it is worthwhile trying to align your values and actions with those of the consumers in your target country.

AUSTRALIA

In Australia, the Global Slavery Index estimates that there are about 15,000 slaves, which is an 11,000 increase over an estimated 4,000 slaves just one year earlier. The statistic isn't meant to imply that there are more slaves now than there were just one year ago. Instead, it highlights how research methodology is catching up with the hidden realities.

Slavery largely flies under the radar, and can be extremely difficult to detect (the mental image of a shackled slave doesn't exist in real life). In fact, the Australian Federal Police only received 170 referrals of human trafficking and slavery-related offences in 2017, and of those only 20% were related to labour conditions. Such a low number of reports reveals how difficult it is to address an incident of slavery, and it is in stark contrast to the much larger number of actual slavery cases that occur throughout Australia.

In addition to the estimated slaves already here, there is also an inestimable number involved offshore in supply chains producing goods for Australian and other consumers.

AN AUSTRALIAN AGRIBUSINESS COMPANY

A major Australian agri/food producer and marketeer – growing, processing and selling over 30 brands in more than 50 countries – has a very international outlook and is subject to many international trends and developments.

Having divisions internationally and with a heavy presence in Asia, from where a significant volume is also sourced, this business is facing increased pressure from consumers and clients in the domestic market as well as in the international market.

Being a supplier to a major US food company producing breakfast products in Australia, and wanting to capture this client globally as well, there was increasing pressure and a building business case for embracing a sustainable supply chain.

The first step taken to develop and implement was to identify category risk profiles. This was done by developing a risk heat map across the categories. The outcome of this allowed the business to select which risks to focus on.

Another sustainable supply chain issue looked into was country of origin, where a process was needed for governance and in regards to deciding what countries to source bulk product from. Developing a method where the business could go through a defined process allowed for a documented, objective and accountable process; that is, why should/shouldn't they maintain a presence in Vietnam? Or why should/shouldn't the business open in Myanmar?

Signing up to the UN Global Compact allowed the business to demonstrate its seriousness to its partners. It also set the clock ticking for producing meaningful reporting, which created a pressure for collecting data. As a further benefit, the target client is also a UN GC signatory, making the reporting almost 'plug 'n' play' for the target client's statement.

Domestically, Australia is stepping up its oversight of slavery issues, and on 28 June 2018 the Australian Federal Government introduced its *Modern Slavery Bill 2018*, which requires more attention to this issue from companies that do business in Australia. Most notably, it requires companies to report publicly where and how slavery is involved in their supply chain and what they are doing to mitigate it:

- The law applies to companies with an annual Australian turnover of over A$100 million.

- The Act expands the definition of 'slavery' to include eight types of extreme exploitation of humans: trafficking in persons; slavery; servitude; forced marriage; forced labour; debt bondage; deceptive recruiting for labour or services; and the worst forms of child labour.[4]

- Affected businesses are required to report to the government on where they are at risk of having slavery practices within their operations and supply chains, what they are doing to curtail those risks, and whether their actions are effective in reducing or eradicating the activity from their supply chain.

The Act presents challenges. Organisations that knowingly rely on the labour and resource exploitation are not likely to openly confess that, and the general perception has been that it's not a business's responsibility to enforce the rule of law in foreign countries.

Experts, including Human Rights Watch, a human rights watchdog organisation that investigates human rights violations in 90 countries, says that while the Act is a good start, it doesn't go far enough. They recommended dropping the qualifying threshold to A$25 million, requiring a 'systematic evaluation' of the corporate slavery risk, and assigning penalties to companies that fail to address the issue.

THE GAME CHANGER

While slavery has been illegal for many years, the game changer is that corporates can no longer turn a blind eye. From now on they need to report and be transparent, which in turn opens them up to scrutiny and accountability.

Other countries are also increasing the level of scrutiny applied to this issue. Let's take a look.

---

4   https://www.homeaffairs.gov.au/criminal-justice/files/modern-slavery-reporting-entities.pdf

THE UNITED KINGDOM

Australia's Act seeks to manage the issue with a similar level of comprehensiveness as the *Modern Slavery Act 2015* now in force in the UK.

In many ways the Australian law is modelled on the UK legislation, with thresholds for who must report, what the modern slavery statement must address, where it must be disclosed, who must sign it (the board of directors) and what the penalties are. It also contains a so-called TISC (transparency in supply chain) provision.

Anyone sentenced in slavery and human trafficking–related crimes will also be subject to fines, the confiscation of proceeds and assets derived, and paying damages to the victims.

The law applies to any company that does business in the UK, without specifying an amount pertaining to business inside the UK. For Australian companies, this means that for any company above the threshold that has business dealings in the UK, the law applies. These companies must report on their slavery or human trafficking–mitigating activities and prominently publish that information on their website.

THE UNITED STATES

The state of California enacted its *Transparency in Supply Chains Act* in 2012 to mandate that businesses with a global turnover of more than US$100 million that do business in California must publicly disclose to consumers their efforts to '… eradicate slavery and human trafficking from their direct supply chain … '. Compliance requires disclosures related to audits, verifications, certifications, internal accountability and training of employees.

The penalty for violating the Act, however, is fairly lax: the state's Attorney General can file an order to have the company address the practice. Consumers are encouraged to report suspicions.

FRANCE

France is another country applying additional efforts to eradicating slavery by requiring companies to implement plans to prevent such abuses anywhere in their supply chains. Its 2017 *Devoir de Vigilance* law (which translates to 'Duty of Vigilance') creates a mandate to report and requires French companies to take steps to eliminate illegal practices when they find them. The law also encompasses child labour and corruption. France's position follows that of the UN's Guiding Principles on Business and Human Rights, and anticipates that emerging technologies will make implementing and enforcing the policies easier.

Interestingly, Total was the first French company to be subjected to a lawsuit based on this law, in late October 2019 just before finishing editing of this book.[5]

For comparison, the following table illustrates how the scope of application differs, based on different measures. These laws intend to bring this issue out into the open, where ignorance is no longer a valid excuse for not addressing these serious issues.

While Australia is playing catch up – both in terms of legislation and consumer attitude – the other three countries (UK, US and France) are examples of countries where consumer sentiment is driving commercial and legal operating conditions.

The good news is that given the similarities in the scopes of legislation, the process of complying will be easily scalable for global businesses or those harbouring global aspirations.

---

5   Business & Human Rights Resource Centre.

Scope of application

	California	United Kingdom	France	Australia
Year	2012	2015	2017	2019
Act	California Transparency in Supply Chains Act	Modern Slavery Act 2015	Devoir de Vigilance	Modern Slavery Act 2018[6]
Applies to businesses with:	Over US$100 million global turnover and at least $500,000 or 25% of global turnover originating in California	Over £36 million global turnover and doing business in the UK	Over 5,000 employees if HQ located in France OR over 10,000 employees if HQ located elsewhere	Over A$100 million global turnover and doing business in Australia
Aligns with:			UN's Guiding Principles on Business and Human Rights	Modern Slavery Act 2015 (UK)

Comments:

- All acts have reporting requirements and intend to place responsibility for oversight with the board of directors.
- Large corporates are intended to be the drivers of change, so if you are a supplier to a large corporate covered by any of these laws, expect to be asked to supply your information to support your client's reporting requirements.
- Enforcement is still weak, but effectiveness reviews are being conducted.

6   The information in this column is for the *Commonwealth of Australia Modern Slavery Act*. At the time of writing, the *NSW Slavery Act* has passed Parliament, but has been sent back to the NSW Legislative Council's Standing Committee for Social Issues for review and possible amendment, and will not be enforced until these last hurdles have been cleared.

GUANGDONG CHILD LABOUR CASE

Working with a shoe factory near Guangzhou, we came upon a table in the glue station with 12 workers around three sides of the table, applying glue to the soles of the shoes being produced. The process started at one corner, before moving around clockwise to the opposite corner, where the table was located adjacent to a conveyor belt, transporting the soles on to the next processing station.

At the corner was clearly a child, participating in the work. On closer inspection, he stated that he was 12 years old. The explanation was clear: the child's father was the worker sitting next to the child, and as it was school holidays, he had taken his son to work to earn some money to help support the family.

Checking that the local school was indeed on holiday, and that the child was under the parental guidance of his legal guardian, it was clear this was an isolated incident rather than a symptom of systematic exploitation.

While this situation would have been frequently seen just 30 years ago in many European countries, it is still a non-compliant situation, and must be stopped, to protect other children where the case is not as easily distinguishable.

As this case was not a 'real' case of child labour, and hence slavery, we reported the known facts to the client in Europe, and let them make their decision on the course of action. In this case, the course of action was to educate the factory managers on what was permissible, and how to uphold the minimum standards of operations.

Due to the layout of the factory, where the street entry gate was at one end of the compound and the entry to the production facilities was right inside the gate, workers would quickly be at their stations in the morning (this particular factory did not operate a dormitory, so all workers stayed outside the premises).

The factory management, offices and showroom were located at the opposite end, down the back of the compound, where the car park was also located. Most of the management team would drive their cars down the back, never looking inside the actual factory, and hence not being aware of who was on the production line unless they had a specific reason to go and look.

In a sense, the management had delegated managing the compliance requirements to line managers, who had no clue or understanding of child labour issues. Similarly, the guard at the street entry didn't stop the child from entering, as it was 'normal' to him.

In short, it was our assessment that this situation arose as a result of the factory general manager not adequately training the team below him to understand what the requirements were. There was no need to take steps to carry out a full-scale child labour remediation case in this instance. The indicators were there, but the situation wasn't clear cut enough that we could make out judgement without significant additional investigations to rule our 'real' child labour as opposed to 'unintentional' child labour.

THE GROWING DEMAND FOR SUSTAINABLE BUSINESS PRACTICES

Not only is it not good business to maintain or give in to unethical practices, the demand for more appropriate business practices is growing in the supply chain. This is termed 'sustainable supply chain management' (SSCM).

Demand from consumers

Companies that have made the switch to more sustainable supply chain policies and practices are often rewarded with a larger potential customer base, especially among younger and activist consumers. The Millennial generation – those born between 1981 and 1997 – is the fastest growing population of consumers, numbering approximately two billion globally as of summer 2018. Making up more than one-quarter of the world's population, this generation is already changing how the world does business. As older generations retire, this group will become even more critical to corporate success in their roles as consumers, workers, and – eventually – leaders. With its youngest members reaching their twenties, the choices and preferences of global Millennials will have immense significance to global business opportunities.

Australia is home to over five million Millennials, who comprise approximately 22% of its population and account for one-third of the workforce. According to the 2018 Deloitte Millennial Survey, this generation is growing increasingly alarmed about several global concerns. While terrorism and incidents of international violence are top of their minds, climate change, sustainability and social inequities follow close behind. And they're not enthusiastic about how today's corporate leadership has prioritised its goals, believing that, in too many cases, the bottom line is prioritised over workers, societies and the environment.

It's not surprising then that Millennials express their dismay through their purchasing habits. According to a 2015 survey of 1,003 American Millennials (500 males; 503 females), a startling nine out of ten (91%) said they'd switch brands to one associated with a 'cause', and almost two in three (62%) said they'd take a pay cut to work for a responsible company. Further:

- more than half indicated their purchasing decisions are influenced by concerns about climate change (59%), biodegradability (62%) and renewable resources (57%)

- almost half (47%) consider greenhouse gas emissions

- more than one in three consider supply chain sustainability (38%) and fair-trade practices (37%).

It's a fair assumption that these numbers will be mirrored in Australia, so if your target market includes any percentage of Millennials, these statistics show how important it is to your business that your supply chain practice becomes and remains as ethical, transparent and honest as possible.

Demand from supply chain partners

As the legal developments noted above indicate, any supply chain member can be held accountable for the omissions of other members. As a consequence, many producers now require their up-chain suppliers – those that contribute to the production and distribution of materials, parts and products – to not only avoid unethical practices but, where legally required, also report their compliance activities. In doing so, they protect the interests of their down-chain partners – those who purchase the end products and goods. With new, more stringent legislation, this is expected to become more prevalent and – eventually – a condition of doing business.

Companies that want to compete internationally will increasingly meet such requirements because it is a sign of good governance, and those further down the chain will not be able to live up to their reporting obligations without adequate information. Initiating this process voluntarily to be ahead of the pack when those mandates finally arrive is a matter of foresight and getting started on the learning curve sooner rather than later.

In the end, and despite the challenges that arise in pursuit of this goal, the decision to become more ethically aware and sustainable is healthy for any business, its customers and the planet on which we live.

THE BENEFITS OF ACTIVE SUSTAINABLE SUPPLY CHAIN MANAGEMENT

It encourages consumer confidence

Consumers are attaching ever-greater importance to sustainability and ethical business conduct as a prime feature of their preferred vendors and suppliers, and many now consider it to be a fundamental component of a healthy business. Companies seeking to win consumer confidence are learning that they must be able to not just maintain an ethical and sustainable supply chain, but also prove it through data and documentation. More consumers are selecting to do business with an ethical enterprise when given a choice between a product from a 'clean' shop versus one that can't demonstrate its commitment to human dignity.

It builds sustainable business partnerships

More corporations now also require their suppliers and partners to take the high road on this subject. You are who you associate with, and this is also true for businesses. Suppliers are expected to know what's going on further down the supply chain, and to ensure that everything practically feasible has been done to mitigate any adverse impacts further down the supply chain. If problematic issues surface it will taint the reputation of the company and its partners. To bolster confidence, many businesses now require their down-chain partners to provide proof of their assertions in easily verifiable formats so they can plug that data into their own systems as evidence of their own mitigating activities.

It makes good business sense

There is a growing group of consumers willing to pay extra for sustainable products, which on its own merits action.

Further, greater transparency in the supply chain also makes business sense by clearly demonstrating to all interested parties the company's openness and attention to good governance as an asset of corporate value. The greater the level of transparency your company presents, the better your oversight of its operations will be, all of which will contribute to better management practices across departments – and not just from an ethical perspective. In effect, sustainability can be used as a driver for change, in more broad terms.

It attracts more investments

An increasing number of investors and investment funds have established 'sustainability' as a criterion for all their potential assets. Companies that transparently communicate their policies and activities and that have a documented process which clearly demonstrates their results will be ahead when it comes to securing funding and/or when supporting the share price, compared to those that can't share the same level of information. And, as the world becomes more sensitive to this issue, scrutiny of unethical business practices for investment purposes is likely to increase.

It highlights company standards

Proactively asserting ethical business practices and policies communicates company values to the workforce, partners, and customers. The improved level of information can help drive a positive team spirit and generate positive worker goodwill. Companies that have clearly articulated and documented their standards on this issue are often also ranked high on 'employer of choice' lists, as well as enjoying a better than average staff retention rate, giving better access to a larger candidate pool who are engaged and motivated as a result of shared values.

* * *

These are just a few of the possible benefits to a business aiming to become sustainable. There are countless others for the participants in the supply chain, including workers and people living in the environment where the product is being manufactured.

4. PREPARING

HOW TO GET STARTED

While the process of creating and maintaining an ethical and sustainable supply chain may seem daunting to begin with, pursuing the goal will result in improved business conditions and long-term company health, making it worthwhile.

Further, once you've clarified and implemented your new sustainable culture and practices, you can start broadcasting it – registering your company in the Sustainability Disclosure Database maintained by the Global Reporting Initiative (GRI) announces to the world both your intentions and actions towards remaining sustainable. Currently, 70 Australian companies are registered with GRI and have submitted 301 reports.

Define your objectives

To understand your end goal, you must first determine where you need to begin. Consider your drivers, and clarify why shifting to more sustainable practices is of value to you and your business. Your goals could include:

- landing a new client who must have clarity on your ability to minimise their risk
- aligning company policies with the sustainability requirements of valued customers
- pleasing potential investors and super funds/pension funds
- improving staff retention
- becoming an employer of choice.

Or, any other motivation, including combinations of several motives.

Note that most companies settle for somewhere in between 'doing business as usual' and 'doing good'. They want something that is both practical and practically achievable.

A SUSTAINABLE SUPPLY CHAIN MANAGEMENT FRAMEWORK

Based on my experience, it is important not to attempt to boil the ocean. It's better to start small and create a solid foundation by establishing a framework. You can then expand on the framework elements as your capacity increases, without having to start over.

There are four distinct stages that it is wise to go through:

1. preparing
2. defining
3. implementing
4. monitoring and evaluating.

If you are starting out, these stages will overlap, and sometimes you will have to go back to make changes because your assumptions weren't correct. This is normal.

In this chapter we will look at preparation, and then we will consider the other three stages in the following chapters.

AN AUSTRALIAN SUPERMARKET CHAIN

A major Australian supermarket chain realised they had an issue in regards to seasonal fruit and vegetable picking. Pickers are often students or, in some cases, people brought in on a scheme from low-wage countries, such as Malaysia, Thailand, China or elsewhere, arriving on tourist visas, often working more hours than a full-time job, and frequently overstaying their visas and being moved around by the people behind the scheme – often labour hire companies operating in a grey zone.

In many cases, the pickers are also 'responsible' for fees, living expenses and travel costs, quickly accumulating debts beyond their salaries, essentially putting them into debt bondage. Or in other words, they are slaves.

Addressing this issue requires knowledge of what is going on out in the field, so establishing oversight over this problem is difficult.

When they reflexively defaulted to the 'audit, audit, audit' position, it was advised they should first get a clear view of the situation, scan the environment for tools and help, and in general take a more structured approach to solving this problem.

A pilot program was established, based on the UK standard 'Clearview', and conducted on a few select sites, and the knowledge gained was used to further develop a response to seasonal labour exploitation in rural farm and fruit picking jobs.

WHERE ARE YOU NOW?

Firstly, it is necessary to understand where you are at. For this stage you cannot start too small, as it could mean overlooking one or more areas that should have been included. I usually suggest starting the process with an assessment of capabilities and gaps, understanding the external operating environment and materiality, and getting a good baseline.

Assess capabilities and identify gaps

For the purpose of assessing the current state, it is useful to use a format such as a capability maturity assessment model, adapted for the purpose of developing a sustainable supply chain.

Assessing areas such as governance, leadership, culture, skills, and metrics can be a real eye-opener if the process has been designed to be honest and asks good questions, such as:

- Does the business have a policy or program regarding a sustainable supply chain?

- Is the program anchored in the governance structure?

- Is it well resourced (financially, personal, technically)?

- Is there a process for risk assessment (related to sustainable supply chain) in place?

- Is it updated regularly?

- Are there any programs in place?

- Do you do any monitoring of suppliers?

- If yes, can it be expanded to include sustainability issues?

- Is it communicated (externally/internally) and are staff trained to handle it adequately?

Answers to these and other questions will form the basis of a maturity rating, as shown opposite.

Maturity ratings

Ad hoc: 1	Processes at this level are (typically) undocumented and in a state of dynamic change, tending to be driven in an ad hoc, uncontrolled and reactive manner.
Repeatable: 2	Some processes are repeatable, possibly with consistent results. Discipline is unlikely to be rigorous, and most processes are undocumented.
Defined: 3	There are sets of defined and documented standard processes established which are subject to some degree of improvement over time, but they may not have been systematically or repeatedly used.
Managed: 4	Effective achievement of the process objectives can be evidenced across a range of operational conditions. The suitability of the process in multiple environments has been tested and the process refined and adapted.
Optimised: 5	Focus is on continually improving process performance through both incremental and innovative technological changes and improvements.

The Capability Maturity Model was originally developed by Carnegie Mellon University.

The external operating environment

I won't go into detail here about understanding the external environment, as we've already considered this in previous chapters. The environment is clearly moving towards a more demanding stage when it comes to being able to demonstrate commitment to sustainability, and a response to that should be considered when developing the sustainability strategy.

Materiality

A sustainable supply chain is a broad concept, and ensuring all aspects are 100% 'squeaky clean' compliant is not a realistic aim to start with. To enable focus and to help with establishing the strategy, it's important to define what are material issues and what are not. Conducting a materiality assessment will help establish priorities.[7]

Baseline

Establishing a baseline of the parameters that should be improved will help you understand where the business is currently at in regard to policies, supplier documentation and other parameters. A baseline is essential for measuring and tracking the results moving forward.

---

7   More information on materiality can be found in chapter 6, Implementing.

5. DEFINING

THE STRATEGY AND ROADMAP

Based on the gaps identified in the preparatory stage, you are in a position to develop a roadmap which will enable closing of the gaps identified.

Again, it's important to break it down into smaller areas and work on what is important and achievable first rather than attempting everything in the first pass. A timeframe of 18 to 24 months for achieving good coverage is reasonable, and should be understood and accepted by all partners and stakeholders.

> In my experience many businesses realise they have a problem before doing the capability assessment, and then have a knee-jerk reaction, throwing themselves at the most obvious solution they can see. In many cases this results in creating an audit or monitoring program. That is a good outcome, but not always the best outcome.

Instead, it's important to understand what the goals are, where the risk is, and what should be done first and what can wait till later.

Key considerations

When defining the strategy, some considerations are universal, while others are industry specific. In the following table are some considerations I consider to be applicable to most industries.

Considerations for most industries

Element	Description
Scope	What is included and what is *not* included is crucial to avoid an open-ended assignment.
	The scope should be defined through the materiality assessment and the strategy.
	The roadmap is how the framework is implemented, within the scope.
Risk criteria	Establish what constitutes acceptable risk related to sustainable supply chain risks.
	This should be addressed through policy-level commitment, defined governance structure and the assignment of resources to a wider risk-management framework.
Alignment of process with other key issues	Ensure there is real alignment and integration of the process to other processes; that is, purchasing, engineering, etc. If not, the result is often an ad hoc approach.
	Integrating this process with other processes, including alignment with sustainability material issues, provides for a better risk-management framework, with less duplication of work.

Element	Description
Develop and implement a due diligence process	A standardised process for evaluating performance of the sustainable supply chain enables like-for-like comparison. By applying a rating system, resources can be better allocated to where the highest risk factors are identified.
Define appropriate actions in the event of unacceptable findings	There must be defined consequences and assigned actions to internal staff in the case that an adverse finding is discovered. Defining consequences and actions means suppliers will be more likely to adhere to the policy, and giving ownership of the process to an inhouse team helps to anchor it.
Develop an internal training program	A formal training structure for ensuring that values are aligned internally is helpful. A calibrated and measured response can be assured.
Ongoing monitoring	An ongoing monitoring program of the supply chain should be in place, to ensure that the due diligence results were and remain acceptable. An ongoing supply chain risk-monitoring program ensures that developing risks can be spotted early and addressed before becoming too costly to mitigate.
Geography	Location of overseas suppliers is a factor largely outside of any business influence. Considering country risk factors is crucial to developing a successful policy.
Product	Product category is another factor to be considered; for example, agricultural products will have an entirely different risk profile to packaging materials, even if both are sourced in the same country.
Depth of process	Depth of process should be considered to define resource usage against the level of risk, and what is reasonable in terms of resources used to mitigate an issue.

ALIGNMENT TO OTHER PROCESSES

For the Sustainable Supply Chain Management Framework to be operational and useful in relation to:

- risk

- legal

- compliance

- procurement

- engineering

- HR/L&D departments

… and not create duplicate or additional workflows, it is optimal if the new Sustainable Supply Chain Management Framework and its processes are aligned and integrate with other existing processes.

Globally recognised best practices

A good place to start to avoid duplicate processes and not reinvent the wheel is to sign up for the United Nations Global Compact (UNGC), which provides a framework for companies seeking to develop a sustainable supply chain.

There are 161 countries that have signed the compact and have committed to following its defined 'best practices'. The Global Compact itself consists of 10 principles. The 10 principles can be broken into 17 practical Sustainable Development Goals (SDGs), making them more operational. Industry standards have their own Codes of Conduct (CoC), which usually more or less overlap with the UNGC principles and the SDGs.

To attain the aspirations in the Principles, the SDGs, or CoCs, many companies take outside advice; for example, from standards-setting organisations. These organisations often offer more specific and in-depth interpretations of social compliance practices and can share experiences due to their industry affiliations.

Some of these standard owners offer additional support with policy or implementation questions, and as an example, the United Nations International Labour Organization (ILO) and United Nations Development Programme (UNDP) have numerous programs globally such as the 'BetterWork' or the 'SCORE' programs. However, most offer support, rather than do-it-for-you services.

WHAT *ARE* HUMAN RIGHTS?

Human rights are a set of rights defined by the UN after the Second World War to safeguard the rights of individuals.

> Human rights are rights inherent to all human beings, regardless of race, sex, nationality, ethnicity, language, religion, or any other status. Human rights include the right to life and liberty, freedom from slavery and torture, freedom of opinion and expression, the right to work and education, and many more. Everyone is entitled to these rights, without discrimination.

Source: https://www.un.org/en/sections/issues-depth/human-rights/

While much has been written about human rights – and there are without a doubt more profound explanations – I will offer my interpretation briefly here. I am no lawyer, nor a human rights specialist, so my take on it is from a practical perspective, using my experience in the supply chain and my personal moral compass.

Historical background

The starting point was the Universal Declaration of Human Rights (UDHR), agreed to in 1948 by 48 out of 58 members in the newly formed United Nations. The declaration contained 30 articles related to different rights.

While the document is agreed to by all members, it is a very aspirational document, and it is not legally binding. Because of the nature of the document, a set of additional conventions was developed in the years following the UDHR, to spell out in practical terms what is to be understood, and how it is to be applied. Later, additional principles and texts were developed, most notably the United Nations Guiding Principles on Business and Human Rights (UNGP) and the Sustainable Development Goals (SDGs).

These conventions, once ratified by the individual countries, are legally binding, although the mechanisms to enforce them remain with either local enforcement or – in the case of Europe – at the European Court of Human Rights.

Some countries argue that human rights are an expression of Western ideals of freedom of the individual, rights to democratic participation, and so on. As such, these rights are rarely or only partially accepted and adhered to by countries with other (non-democratic) types of government. In some countries with more focus on the group rather than the individual, and long historical and philosophical traditions, accepting individual rights as being above the group (the state) is hard to accept.

Some of the key rights are:

- freedom from slavery
- freedom of thought
- freedom of opinion
- freedom of religion
- freedom from persecution
- freedom from discrimination
- equal rights to women, children and men.

While there is a tendency to use the different terms a bit arbitrarily, a timeline – and an understanding of what each item is, what its purpose is, and when it was created or came into force – can prove useful when helping to understand the environment in which businesses operate in today.

Timeline

1948	Universal Declaration of Human Rights
1966	The International Covenant on Economic, Social and Cultural Rights (ICESCR) and The International Covenant on Civil and Political Rights (ICCPR)
1976	Bill of Human Rights
1999	United Nations Global Compact
2011	United Nations Guiding Principles on Business and Human Rights
2015	United Nations Sustainable Development Goals (SDGs)

Let's have a look at each of these elements individually.

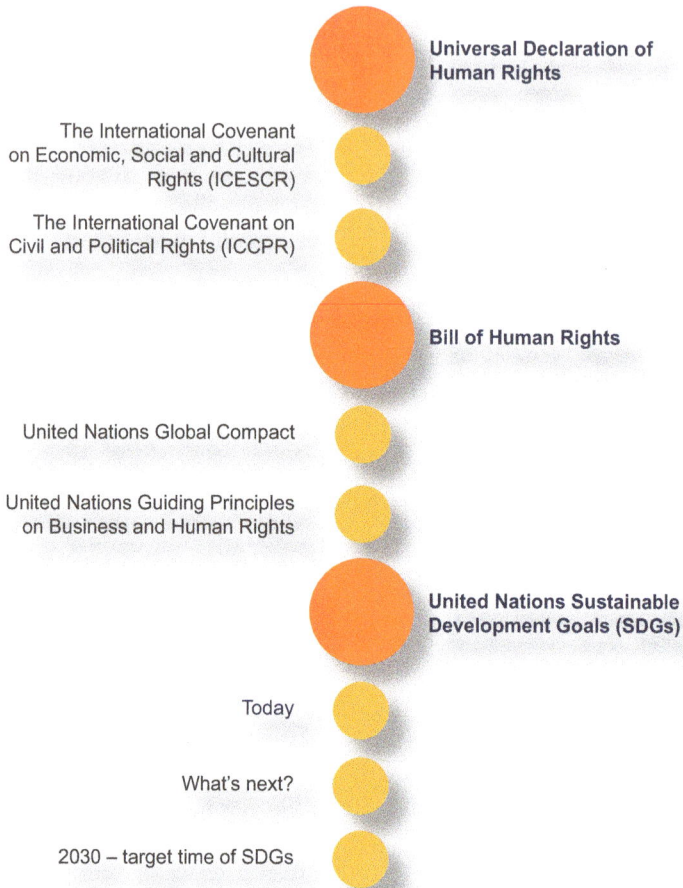

Universal Declaration of
Human Rights

The International Covenant
on Economic, Social and Cultural
Rights (ICESCR)

The International Covenant on
Civil and Political Rights (ICCPR)

Bill of Human Rights

United Nations Global Compact

United Nations Guiding Principles
on Business and Human Rights

United Nations Sustainable
Development Goals (SDGs)

Today

What's next?

2030 – target time of SDGs

Universal Declaration of Human Rights

All human beings are born free and equal in dignity and rights.
They are endowed with reason and conscience and should act
towards one another in a spirit of brotherhood.

Source: United Nations Declaration of Human Rights

The Universal Declaration of Human Rights was written on the ashes of millions of dead and displaced people. It consists of 30 Articles, each being a human right.

The Declaration was first discussed by the United Nations General Assembly in 1946. The drafting committee was chaired by Eleanor Roosevelt, and some drafting committee members argued that the UDHR should not only represent Western ideals, that there may be more than one approach, and that the committee should spend a few months studying Confucianism before settling on the formulation of the text.

The UDHR was adopted by the UN General Assembly on 10 December 1948, which is now International Human Rights Day.

The ICESCR and ICCPR

While the Universal Declaration of Human Rights was a very good starting point, it is largely aspirational, it doesn't contain many practical details, and it is open to interpretation. For this reason, additional conventions, covenants and treaties were needed.

This led to the development of two very important conventions:

- The International Covenant on Economic, Social and Cultural Rights (ICESCR)

- The International Covenant on Civil and Political Rights (ICCPR).

The first covenant focuses on the right to work, social protection, education and cultural freedoms. The second focuses on rights such as free speech, religious freedoms, democratic participation and so forth.

The Bill of Human Rights

The Bill of Human Rights was originally envisioned as consisting of the Universal Declaration of Human Rights, the ICCPR and ICESCR in a combined covenant, and a guide on Measures of Implementation.

```
                    ┌──────────────────┐
                    │ The International │
                    │   Covenant on    │
                    │ Civil and Political │
                    │      Rights      │
                    └──────────────────┘
                              │
                              ▼
┌──────────────┐      ╭──────────────╮      ┌──────────────────┐
│  Universal   │      │    Bill of   │      │ The International │
│ Declaration of │──▶ │ Human Rights │ ◀──  │   Covenant on    │
│ Human Rights │      │              │      │ Economic, Social │
└──────────────┘      ╰──────────────╯      │   and Cultural   │
                                            │      Rights      │
                                            └──────────────────┘
```

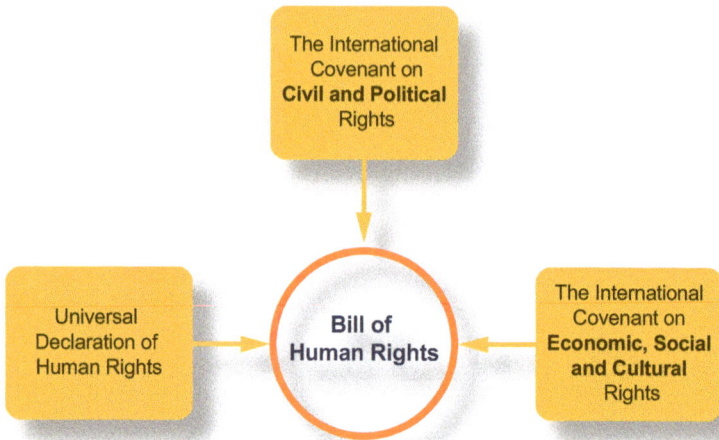

With nations of the world descending into the Cold War, China closing itself off and other limiting developments preventing progress as originally envisioned, the original covenant was split and the measures of implementation fell by the wayside. This may explain why so many additional treaties, covenants and principles had to be developed subsequently.

The United Nations Global Compact

The United Nations Global Compact was created in 1999, and it is the single largest corporate social responsibility initiative with over 10,000 business members and approximately 3,000 non-business members globally, spread over 170 countries.

It is a principles-based network open to businesses, organisations and cities, aimed at promoting responsible business behaviour. The UNGC is based on 10 principles, related to human rights, labour, the environment and fighting corruption.

Membership is relatively low priced, and it requires that the member issue a Communication on Progress (COP) every year. This is to be uploaded to the UNGC website and is publicly available in the UNGC searchable database. At the time of writing, members have submitted almost 65,000 COP reports. The sheer number of COPs being prepared and submitted every year indicates how this is becoming mainstream, and there are many examples of this being incorporated into procurement decision-making processes.

If you have clients who are UNGC members, it is worth considering if your business should also join, enabling you to provide a COP which, if it is of a sufficiently high quality, will almost 'plug and play' into your clients' COP, making their life easier.

Depending on where in the process you and your clients are, this can either be an early-mover competitive advantage or, at the very least, not an impediment to securing that crucial business relationship.

THE 10 UNGC PRINCIPLES

Human rights:

1. Businesses should support and respect the protection of internationally proclaimed human rights; and

2. Make sure that they are not complicit in human rights abuses.

Labour:

3. Businesses should uphold the freedom of association and the effective recognition of the right to collective bargaining;

4. The elimination of all forms of forced and compulsory labour;

5. The effective abolition of child labour; and

6. The elimination of discrimination in respect of employment and occupation.

Environment:

7. Businesses should support a precautionary approach to environmental challenges;

8. Undertake initiatives to promote greater environmental responsibility; and

9. Encourage the development and diffusion of environmentally friendly technologies.

Anti-corruption:

10. Businesses should work against corruption in all its forms, including extortion and bribery.

Source: https://www.unglobalcompact.org

The United Nations Guiding Principles on Business and Human Rights

These principles were adopted on 16 June 2011, and are often referred to as the 'Ruggie Principles' after the Special Representative of the Secretary-General John Ruggie, who oversaw their development. They are the first principles developed to help businesses address human rights in their approach to conducting their activities.

The United Nations Guiding Principles on Business and Human rights consist of three pillars, shown in the following table.

Protect	Respect	Remedy
States have a duty to protect.	Businesses have a responsibility to respect.	People affected by business-related abuse, must have access to remedy.

The pillars define the responsibilities of governments and businesses, and give affected people the right to a remedy. There are 31 Principles, and it's the first corporate human rights framework to be endorsed by the United Nations.

The following two principles out of the 31 show how businesses should recognise human rights and how due diligence is a must when dealing with human rights violations.

Principle 12: Foundational Principles	Principle 17: Human rights due diligence
The responsibility of business enterprises to respect human rights refers to internationally recognized human rights – understood, at a minimum, as those expressed in the International Bill of Human Rights and the principles concerning fundamental rights set out in the International Labour Organization's Declaration on Fundamental Principles and Rights at Work.	In order to identify, prevent, mitigate and account for how they address their adverse human rights impacts, business enterprises should carry out human rights due diligence. The process should include assessing actual and potential human rights impacts, integrating and acting upon the findings, tracking responses, and communicating how impacts are addressed. Human rights due diligence:
	(a) Should cover adverse human rights impacts that the business enterprise may cause or contribute to through its own activities, or which may be directly linked to its operations, products or services by its business relationships;
	(b) Will vary in complexity with the size of the business enterprise, the risk of severe human rights impacts, and the nature and context of its operations;
	(c) Should be ongoing, recognizing that the human rights risks may change over time as the business enterprise's operations and operating context evolve.

Source: Report of the Special Representative of the Secretary-General on the issue of human rights and transnational corporations and other business enterprises, John Ruggie

The United Nations Guiding Principles on Business and Human Rights provide excellent guidance on how businesses should go about implementing adequate measures to prevent human rights abuses in their business and their sphere of influence – including the supply chain – without having to encroach on what should be up to governments to enforce. (The required laws are often in existence, but are often poorly enforced.)

The United Nations Sustainable Development Goals

The SDGs contain 17 goals, and if you haven't done so already it's a good start to align your strategy to the SDGs.

The 2030 Agenda for Sustainable Development, adopted by all United Nations Member States in 2015, provides a shared blueprint for peace and prosperity for people and the planet, now and into the future. At its heart are the 17 Sustainable Development Goals (SDGs), which are an urgent call for action by all countries – developed and developing – in a global partnership. They recognize that ending poverty and other deprivations must go hand-in-hand with strategies that improve health and education, reduce inequality, and spur economic growth – all while tackling climate change and working to preserve our oceans and forests.

Source: https://sustainabledevelopment.un.org/?menu=1300

Often the goals are referred to in their more condensed form:

1. No poverty
2. Zero hunger
3. Good health and wellbeing
4. Quality education

5. Gender equality

6. Clean water and sanitation

7. Affordable and clean energy

8. Decent work and economic growth

9. Industry, innovation and infrastructure

10. Reduced inequalities

11. Sustainable cities and communities

12. Responsible consumption and production

13. Climate action

14. Life below water

15. Life on land

16. Peace, justice and strong institutions

17. Partnerships for the goals

However, the goals are much more granular than that. Below is the text from the United Nations website, but each of the goals has sub-goals, or more granular actions to be implemented to reach the overall goals.

Goal 1	End poverty in all its forms everywhere
Goal 2	End hunger, achieve food security and improved nutrition and promote sustainable agriculture
Goal 3	Ensure healthy lives and promote wellbeing for all at all ages
Goal 4	Ensure inclusive and equitable quality education and promote lifelong learning opportunities for all
Goal 5	Achieve gender equality and empower all women and girls

Goal 6	Ensure availability and sustainable management of water and sanitation for all
Goal 7	Ensure access to affordable, reliable, sustainable and modern energy for all
Goal 8	Promote sustained, inclusive and sustainable economic growth, full and productive employment and decent work for all
Goal 9	Build resilient infrastructure, promote inclusive and sustainable industrialization and foster innovation
Goal 10	Reduce inequality within and among countries
Goal 11	Make cities and human settlements inclusive, safe, resilient and sustainable
Goal 12	Ensure sustainable consumption and production patterns
Goal 13	Take urgent action to combat climate change and its impacts
Goal 14	Conserve and sustainably use the oceans, seas and marine resources for sustainable development
Goal 15	Protect, restore and promote sustainable use of terrestrial ecosystems, sustainably manage forests, combat desertification, and halt and reverse land degradation and halt biodiversity loss
Goal 16	Promote peaceful and inclusive societies for sustainable development, provide access to justice for all and build effective, accountable and inclusive institutions at all levels
Goal 17	Strengthen the means of implementation and revitalize the global partnership for sustainable development

For additional information, each goal has been broken down into even more detailed steps on the website: https://sustainabledevelopment.un.org/post2015/transformingourworld

Aligning your materiality assessment to the SDGs helps to steer the efforts applied, and provides alignment between what is important to you and what is important to the community. For example, at a water utility, SDG 6: Clean water and sanitation would be obvious, while for a retailer, SDG 8: Decent work and economic growth could (would) be an obvious choice.

The SDGs have 12 sub-goals (or targets), and the UN partners work with various governments, NGOs and businesses to implement change that will drive the achievement of the overall goal. For example, SDG 8 has over 1,000 partnerships globally, including with ministries, governments, societies and businesses, all striving to meet Goal 8.

Sustainable Development Goal 8.7

Because of the focus of this book, and my personal interest in modern slavery, a special mention must be given to SDG 8.7 – because this clause focuses on forced labour and slavery.

8 DECENT WORK AND ECONOMIC GROWTH

SDG 8.7 states that we all must:

Take immediate and effective measures to eradicate forced labour, end modern slavery and human trafficking and secure the prohibition and elimination of the worst forms of child labour, including recruitment and use of child soldiers, and by 2025 end child labour in all its forms.

The key here is that if we are to achieve this goal, many other elements must be in place. If people do not have choices, they are more susceptible to exploitation because they cannot afford to uphold the level of scepticism required to steer clear of human traffickers, slave traders, and deceptive recruiters.

The good thing is that Goal 1 aims to end poverty by 2030, at which stage the other goals would have to have been solved as well to claim success. While I have some doubts about achieving that in this timeframe, I have no doubt that we must try.

A FURNITURE FACTORY NEAR NINGBO, ZHEJIANG PROVINCE

A young worker was found to be working in the factory. It was verified that this worker had recently turned 16 (young workers in China are defined as 16 to 18 years old). Below 16 years of age is considered child labour in China.

This worker had been working in the factory prior to her birthday, meaning that the factory had employed child labour. The factory had upwards of 500 employees, and only one young worker was found. After validating some other young workers onsite, it was evident that several workers had been employed prior to being of legal working age.

The factory didn't employ the relevant free resources available to validate the ID cards of workers, or in other words had no process in place to ensure child labour was not occurring. This may not have been a deliberate act, but most definitely it was a management oversight.

The remediation was to help the factory implement a process whereby all workers had their ID cards checked on the government website upon starting work, and records were kept for future audit purposes.

It was a simple solution, and it rules out non-intentional child labour risks for the factory.

WHAT IS THE ROLE OF A BUSINESS IN RELATION TO HUMAN RIGHTS?

The role of a business in human rights is limited to its own operations and those of its business partners. It is not the business's responsibility to take on the duty of the state, although in some cases the delineation between the two can seem porous and interpretation must be applied.

Some organisations are to an extent encroaching on the duties of the state – especially in countries where enforcement is lax or non-existent due to corruption and other unethical practices.

Policies required for businesses

As in any other area of a well-managed business, policies and procedures are necessary in the area of sustainable supply chain management, and in fact the entire business can benefit if the work to update the portfolio of policies makes an effort to integrate the policies related to corporate social responsibility, sustainability, sustainable supply chain and modern slavery.

Generally, businesses should have a:

- human rights policy

- remediation policy

- supplier code of conduct

- procurement policy

- environmental policy

- whistleblower policy

- anti-money laundering policy

- anti-bribery and corruption policy.

Some policies are legislated for all businesses, and some are compulsory for particular types of business operations or locations; for example, an offshore oil exploration company must have an environmental policy dealing with preventing risks, as well as a mitigation plan in the event of an oil spill. Others are simply good practice and part of a strong governance system.

As a minimum, a company that's serious about demonstrating they are worthy of their social licence to operate should have a human rights policy. A human rights policy could simply refer to (and state the business is committed to working to promote) the United Nations Guiding Principles on Human Rights, or it could be an independently developed document.

An advantage of referring to the United Nations Guiding Principles is that this is a generally accepted and acknowledged standard and level of commitment. A disadvantage is that the principles are entirely out of your control and influence. You cannot alter, reduce or be selective in your commitment.

An independent human rights policy gives more freedom and flexibility to meet your business's needs, but also provides less stature in the community.

When addressing modern slavery and sustainable supply chains, a human rights policy is a bare minimum, because it will provide the minimum standard against which to measure and improve.

Other than the human rights policy, various codes of conduct and policies are necessary. For example, an anti-money laundering policy is important, because money laundering and slavery often go hand in hand.

It is possible to develop a more generic Standard of Business Conduct (SoBC) including all of these policies, and in fact that is probably advisable in many cases, but it is also easy to fall into the trap that compiling these policies into a comprehensive document may make the SoBC very lengthy reading.

The key with the policies is to not trap the entire business in an impossible-to-navigate web of policies, rules, regulations and red tape, so a proper balance must be struck to allow efficient operations to continue without unnecessary impediments.

GOOD GOVERNANCE

ESG, sustainability and governance

ESG (environmental, social and corporate governance) and CSR (corporate social responsibility) are largely the same issues, but looked at from different perspectives.

ESG is the term used by, for example, the board of directors, the C-suite, investors, and anybody involved with any degree of business management and reporting. It is an umbrella term covering the business's approach to environment, social and governance and how it goes about doing its business.

CSR (or sustainability, or one of the many other names this area goes by) is also about environmental and social issues, and governance is covered by how the environmental and social strategies are put into force, by means of programs, projects, partnerships, and how they are managed (governed).

When I say they are the same, it is because you can't have one without the other; that is, unless the activity is pure window dressing. In a sense, you can say that ESG is the measurement of the application of the CSR efforts a business is undertaking to improve their operations and reputation.

The goal of implementing all these steps (other than improving the lives and sustainability of the people and the environment affected by your supply chain) is to provide some tangible results, translated into ESG measures to management. These measures work to improve governance, reduce risk, or capture opportunities. To achieve that, whatever project, program or partnership is developed and implemented must be measurable.

ESG scoping

When it comes to scoring a company based on its sustainability performance (ESG performance), a range of factors must be included. Aligning how the business is being operated according to these factors will – if done right – yield a better score, which ultimately could be reflected in the share price or in the rates obtained on, for example, green bonds.

An assessment of a business could look like this:

Area	Environmental	Social	Governance	TOTAL
Internal				
External				
Weighted/ tilted				
Change over past performance				
Total				

Ensuring that alignment across all areas of ESG is balanced allows you to feel more confident that you are covered. Similarly, ensuring you have the right balance of internal and external measures in combination with a reasonable weighting/tilt and documented change over past years helps to increase the percentage of managed risks over unmanaged risks, which in turn reduces the risk of being blindsided by issues that could have been managed.

ESG measurement

To provide comparative and qualitative analytics, there are several ESG rating tools.

Some attempt to rate the management proficiency of a business, taking it as a proxy for how professionally a business is run. This then is used as a proxy for how effectively a CSR program is being run or introduced, which also may be assessed by proxy measurements.

The hypothesis behind this approach is good, because we do know that strong governance produces better results. However, proxies of proxies do need a robust on-the-ground due diligence program that allows for a calibration of the different tiers of proxies and their accuracy at measuring what they were intended to measure.

Some benchmark across industries while others benchmark taking into account what is in the news and what is available via other information sources, such as the US 'Trafficking in Persons Report' (TiP) or based on other industry characteristics.

While the idea of measuring something which often is intangible is good, the outcome is never more than an indicator of what happened in the past, along with some aspirations for the future. As a proxy, it is at best indirect, and at worst it can be a false measure.

ESG ratings companies

There are several reputable ESG ratings companies, using slightly different measuring methodologies. Some of the more well-known ones are Sustainalytics, MSCI, RepRisk and Refinitiv (Thomson Reuters).

They all have access to deep datasets originating in their original core business, and as the need has arisen, ESG ratings evolved out of the core businesses. For example, MSCI's rankings are based on a range of data on ESG policies, programs, performance, as well as data on over 65,000 directors and more than 13 years of shareholder meeting results. To filter the ratings based on industry, an additional 37 key issues allow for both general and specific ratings.

Sustainalytics base their ratings on five overall factors: innovation, materiality, granularity, comparability and a dynamic weighting.

Refinitiv, while independent from former parent company Thomson Reuters, still heavily relies on information from Thomson Reuters, and as such probably has a more traditional approach; for example, including financial crimes information in their assessments.

While these ESG ratings platforms all have their strengths, considering the slight differences, any large corporate relying on ESG ratings to support their share price or financiers providing capital at a favourable price should ensure that their efforts support their ESG scores at a good level, not just with one platform, but across as many as possible.

At the end of the day, in my experience the most important issue is how much of the total risk is managed and how much isn't.

Why? Because there are only two options: pull back, and have no risk to manage – which is unrealistic, because it also implies discontinuation of the business. The other option is to better manage or reduce the overall proportion of unmanaged risk. This is, however, complicated because unmanaged risk tends to be more complex risk, with the additional twist that any potentially fallout can be very large.

In my experience, the managed risk often tends to be the risk that can be measured directly; for example, CO_2 emissions, resource usage and other issues that can be easily 'engineered'.

Following the mantra 'what gets measured gets managed', the unmanaged risk is often the 'too-hard' issues, which also often sit in the social area; for example, human rights, social compliance and social impact, and stakeholder engagement. This also happens to be the area where modern slavery sits, which highlights how hard a topic it is to manage. This of course doesn't mean that it shouldn't be attempted.

ESG, the board, and where the buck stops

While CSR is the responsibility of the operations of a business, ESG is the board's responsibility. From a board perspective it's an opportunity to reduce the risk profile, capture new profit lines and make the business and its share price more resilient to shocks. Giving it proper attention is and should be part of the board's fiduciary duty to shareholders – similar to the Hutley Opinion on Climate Change and Directors' Duties, eventually this opinion could (and should) be expanded to cover social risks as well.[8]

Giving this issue proper attention along with all the other items on a board's agenda is no easy task, but it is gaining more traction at the moment. The best approach a board can take is to ensure the policies are adequate, properly implemented, and that the outcomes are monitored.

Policies

Policies have been covered on pages 61 and 62, but just briefly, it's important that the board, executive committee or C-suite is part of formulating the policies, especially in regards to setting targets, because that ensures better implementation. Or, in other words, it strengthens the 'governance' part of ESG.

Additionally, often middle management is trying to second guess what the board is prepared to accept in terms of ambitions and targets, outside the traditional areas of sales and profit goals and risk appetite.

---

8   The Centre for Policy Development and the Future Business Council; Climate
     Change and Directors' Duties – Legal Opinion.

If that second guessing is based on misunderstandings or unclear communication lines, the practical implementation is skewed and often even jeopardised.

Implementation

Implementation is – as always – about resources. Are there sufficient specialist resources internally to properly implement the strategy behind the policies? Considering that these are specialist skills, it makes sense to go external for some assistance, simply because this function is not required on a full-time basis at most companies. Can it be bolted onto another function; for example, corporate communications, legal or procurement? Yes, of course it can, however the team being tasked with the implementation isn't necessarily strong in this particular skill-set, hence the quality of the outcome may not be entirely up to the level required. Additionally, this type of staff may not have a particular interest in performing this role, and hence motivation becomes another factor to be considered.

A general data-gathering program – that is, an audit program on suppliers in far-away production facilities – can be easily set up and managed, but the key is to know what you are looking for and what pitfalls exist, in case the scope of the program isn't set up correctly.

On a larger scale, capacity building of suppliers, agents and other parts of the supply chain overseas can cause problems of insufficient scale. For example, if you are to implement a supplier capacity-building program in Bangladesh, you often run into problems with the cost of the program being prohibitive if distributed over only a few producers.

To counter this, there are several member-driven organisations that aggregate projects, but you may have a little less direct influence over what is being done.

Oversight

Oversight can be carried out in many ways: in person, by delegate or by proxy. Realistically, it is difficult to expect the board to inspect suppliers, but oversight includes that there is follow up and that either a company delegate or an assigned proxy has visited some of the suppliers deemed to pose a higher degree of risk.

By ensuring there is such a program in place, it is harder to argue that the board hasn't lived up to its fiduciary duties.

The board has an obligation not to mislead in the statements issued by the principal governing body of a business. Laws in most countries include clauses to the effect that it is prohibited to give 'false and misleading statements', which translates into the board cannot sign and publish a modern slavery statement without proper due diligence on the supply regime. In effect, a company must inspect at least part of its supply chain, and have a good reason, demonstrating why that particular supplier was chosen over another location.

Having a plan for how to distribute the due diligence efforts is crucial to demonstrate due care and diligence.

Who is responsible?

Who is responsible for policing the outcome and achieving the targets? Is it, for example, the private equity firm owning a majority share, or a merchandiser or buyer, who should spend more on ensuring that the correct policies, procedures and metrics are in place and that sustainability due diligence of at-risk issues is undertaken regularly to control the risk?

A merchandiser/buyer can walk away relatively easily, while – once invested – a private equity firm cannot. To me, that actually answers the question, however until now it would appear that the answer has been the reverse.

Interestingly, it seems that the deeper the engagement is, the less interest there is in ensuring that the ESG performance is up to standard, while those without skin in the game – who have the ability to walk away at any time – are often those who care more. To me, that is a bit odd. I have illustrated this on the following page.

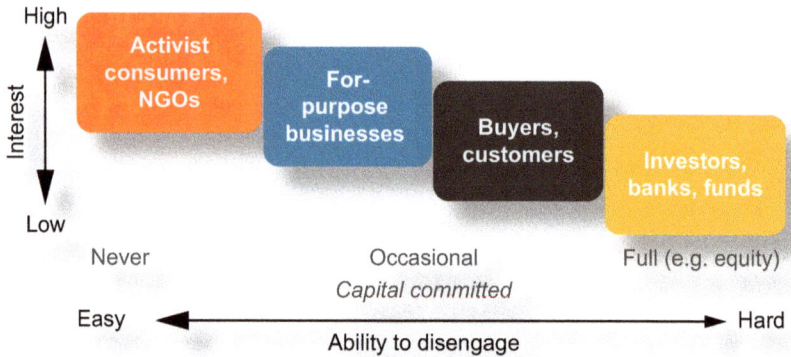

Investors push the responsibility down onto their investment targets, but can they actually trust them, especially when metrics are difficult to establish and it therefore ends up in the 'too-hard basket'?

As an executive compared to an operator, who should have more interest in doing 'enough' to validate the conditions? The person who takes the blame or the person who takes the loss? Ideally, the responsibility is distributed in a balanced fashion. Buyers have an interest in securing the continuity of their business and protecting their brand, while investors have exactly the same objective.

ESG

Environment, Social and Governance, policy level, governance, encompasses everything related to the board's activities and responsibilities, including reporting

CSR

Environmental and Social Sustainability, including governance hereof. It covers mostly practical aspects; that is, projects and program management and implementation

An ESG checklist for boards

1. Define material risks and opportunities and adopt a strategic response to meet the needs of the business.

2. Define three to five KPIs for each area of ESG. Ensure these are balanced and representative of all areas.

3. Define the KPIs according to quantitative and qualitative measures, and make sure the qualitative measures can be converted into a quantitative indicator.

4. Do not neglect 'S', even if it is the hardest to measure. If direct measure is impossible, develop meaningful proxies, and test their relevance on an ongoing basis.

5. Track the KPIs moving forward.

6. Create programs that aim to improve. Working with the supply chain to improve its standards over the longer term is imperative in securing future quality and supplier partnerships when needed.

7. Consider whether green bonds are right for you and your funding needs. Green bonds are another way to access the huge pools of ESG capital and drive shareholder value.

8. Consider aligning your ESG program with, for example, the United Nations 17 Sustainable Development Goals; becoming a member of United Nations Global Compact; or adopting the United Nations Principles on Business and Human Rights, because these are factors fund managers and institutional investors use to evaluate their relationship with your business in regard to your ESG performance.

9. Consider if using external resources to assist with alignment of your policies, processes and programs to external rating companies – such as Sustainalytics and MSCI – could be cost effective and helpful.

10. Consider establishing an external gauge of the program to enable progress measurement, and engage a third party to validate the results and to give your program credibility.

11. Assign accountability for your ESG program to one person, such as general counsel, head of investor relations or the CFO.

12. Define how to access responsible investors and fund managers to tap into the investment community investing in programs that demonstrate good ESG performance.

Questions the board should ask to mitigate risk

Many companies and boards use the 'three lines of defence' framework, to ensure that proper protection is in place to safeguard the business from risks, but in order to use the methodology correctly, you need to ask the right questions.[9]

Having prepared board materials in the past, I know that many subordinates take the approach that the materials presented should never lead to any difficult questions being asked of them. This outcome can be secured two ways:

- by ensuring all bases are 100% covered

- using manipulation, directing the attention of the board in the wrong direction, or even playing to an individual's particular interests, and playing down what is likely to raise a stir.

To avoid being manipulated, it is of utmost importance that the board knows how to validate the information being presented, which will ultimately feed into the ESG scoring. To ensure that proper care and due diligence has gone into the process, the board should ask questions down the reporting line, to validate the findings. The questions

---

9   The three lines of defence is an internal audit model: the 'first line' is own/manage the risk, the 'second line' is oversee the risk (for example, risk management and compliance), and the 'third line' is assurance, normally performed by the internal audit function.

should cover policy, processes and information sources and data accuracy – for example:

Policies:

- Are the policies adequate?

- Are the policies aligned with international and/or recognised standards?

- Do the policies properly reflect what we are rated on in terms of ESG?

Processes and procedures:

- What are the risks? Where are our biggest exposures? How did we arrive at this result?

- Are there defined responsibilities?

- Do the team take time to properly use the risk management frameworks developed?

- Are the processes biased or skewed towards a particular area, and leaving risks of being blindsided to other areas?

- Has proper care and due diligence been exercised?

Information sources/data accuracy:

- How can we be sure that the proxies we use to measure are accurate? What have we done to validate the connections?

- How did you validate this information?

- How confident are you that it is factual, accurate and believable?

- If you had any extra resources available, where would you like to use it? Where would it increase our confidence levels that we are okay with the results?

A simple checklist like the one opposite can be used to ensure the board considers various aspects of ESG 'covered'. What is important is to ask the right questions before accepting or rejecting them. Such questions could cover:

- Are the policies adequate? Do they align with legal requirements?

- Do systems and processes support the policies?

- Is there alignment to the United Nations Global Compact/United Nations Guiding Principles on Business and Human Rights/ United Nations Sustainable Development Goals/ISO20400?

- What outcomes are expected?

- Are the results measurable?

- Has responsibility been assigned for delivery of the results?

- Who is accountable for the result?

- Has external expertise been consulted?

- Are the results assured (full, limited or no assurance)?

- Do you have something to report and are you ready to report?

- Is overall compliance reached?

There are plenty of guides and processes available in hard and soft copy, making it superfluous to reproduce guidance for environment and governance, but where the 'S' of ESG (social) often falls over is it's a new discipline gaining mainstream acceptance faster than the metrics are being developed. Measuring the social aspect of ESG is often more of a qualitative than a quantitative approach. This means you will often be measuring proxies that allow you to develop a KPI system in an area where it's difficult to obtain hard and fast metrics.

Gap identification checklist

Rate each parameter according to a simple score: Good, Medium or Poor.

#	Area	Environment	Social	Governance	Notes
1	Policies	Medium	Poor	Good	...
2	Systems and processes	Good	Poor	Medium	...
3	UNGP/UNGC/UNSDG/ISO20400, etc. alignment	Poor	Medium	Medium	...
4	Defined outcome	Poor	Poor	Poor	...
5	Measurables	Medium	Poor	Medium	...
6	Responsibility assigned	Good	Poor	Medium	...
7	Accountability assigned	Good	Poor	Good	...
8	Consulted (subject matter expert)	Medium	Poor	Good	...
9	Assurance and validation	Poor	Poor	Medium	...
10	Reporting	Medium	Poor	Medium	...
11	Compliant	Poor	Poor	Medium	...

Metrics examples for the board to ensure oversight

While the metrics for slavery are not likely to be very useful, because cases will not be found every second day (hopefully!), proxies and other better measures that can be used to reflect ongoing changes must be developed. These could include:

- due diligence, monitoring and inspections – as a percentage of the category volume

- managed risk versus unmanaged risk

- industry benchmarking

- how many factory workers were reached in the supply chain?

- number of supplier visits (visits where you stay in the boardroom do not count!)

- number of minor, major, and critical non-compliances found

- how many suppliers were trained or engaged with?

- how many human rights due diligences were performed?

- how many risk assessments led to actions being taken?

- what was the average time in days from a finding being transformed into a corrective action and being finalised?

- how many labour violations were found?

- how many due diligence findings were identified and how many were corrected?

- were there any apprentice schemes used?

- how many slaves were found?

- what were the changes to the metrics?

These metrics are examples, and others may be more relevant for your business. It's important to have an ability to collect data points at intervals that makes sense for your business and also for the relevant reporting period.

Some people say that 'any slave found should be celebrated', meaning that this person can be helped. I won't go that far, but it is important to be courageous and not stick your head in the sand. Celebrating the development of KPIs and starting to keep track is what matters, because without starting to measure, how will you know what progress you have made?

26 QUESTIONS THAT HELP TO ESTABLISH IF THE PERSON IN FRONT OF YOU HAS PRACTICAL EXPERIENCE

Unfortunately, the consulting industry is not short on 'experts' with little to no relevant practical experience. To an extent, the sustainability consulting industry in Australia suffers from a lack of appropriately qualified experts. And while I am a big advocate of 'transferable skills', experiences that originate 20 to 25 years ago are perhaps not the most relevant to the situation found today.

Taking this type of 'authority' as being the pinnacle of this field possibly demonstrates the buyer inexperience in this area of consulting services.

Being aware of self-proclaimed experts

There is a theory that you need over 10,000 hours of experience to truly master a skill, or in other words to be an 'expert'.

Recently I attended a conference where a prominent person from a leading anti-slavery organisation asked the attendees questions about our experience: 'How many are starting out?', then, 'How many have two or three years' experience', before finishing at up to five years of experience. Perhaps naively, I expected the next question to be '… more than 10 years' experience', but that question never came, as if it was a bit ludicrous to expect anyone in Australia to have 10-plus years of experience in this field.

Well, it's not ludicrous. There are plenty of people here from overseas with even 20-plus years of experience, but because this issue is new in Australia, there is an assumption that anyone with more than two years of experience is an 'expert'. With that perception, it's very easy to make assumptions about the general level of experience and skills available in the market.

There is, however, most certainly a lack of understanding at play here: newbie 'experts' believing they are at the leading edge, but in reality they are nowhere near best practice nor proficient. Unfortunately, these consultants can be a grave danger to the companies that employ them – especially if the efforts are to be scrutinised by overseas customers or investors who have dealt with these issues for much longer, in some cases even decades. The lack of expertise will be obvious.

It doesn't help either that almost every conference held openly states that Australia is 'leading the pack' because we have the *Modern Slavery Act*. But many other countries do not have a modern slavery act because their enforcement of trafficking laws is better and civil society expects action from brands and businesses to receive their hard-earned cash in purchasing transactions.

The biggest danger is that if the consulting industry collectively suffers from the Dunning–Kruger effect, there is almost no need to progress, because we are already there …

As a result of this, as a business you are very susceptible to setting goals unambitiously low and engaging inexperienced staff and consultants, who may be skilled in communicating and sounding very knowledgeable, but have zero practical experience when it comes to setting up systems that create the basis for progress.

A good starting place is to educate yourself to look through the fluff and get some pointers as to whether a given consultant has the skills needed to put a practical, effective program into place. This will enable you to understand their experience and assess if the person in front of you is merely hot air with all the right phrases or is a skilled practitioner.

To achieve this, you can ask the supplier, service provider, consultant, or expert some questions that will enable you to gauge their real level of experience.

Such questions could include:

1. What direction did your initial education take you?

2. What are the typical issues you have seen at factories?

3. How much time do you usually spend in each factory? What do you do when there?

4. How many meetings do you have each day when on a sourcing trip?

5. How many evening or dinner meetings do you normally arrange?

6. Have you ever done a child labour remediation process? Or do you just know about this from a theoretical perspective?

7. If you have practical experience, please explain your personal experience remediating a case of child labour. Explain the situation, what was done, how it was uncovered, and what was done to remediate and prevent.

8. Have you ever uncovered underpayment? How? What did you do to remediate it?

9. What have you done to verify that a factory is not making people work for more than the permissible hours?

10. How many factories have you visited?

11. When was your last time in a factory?

12. How often do you travel there?

13. What are your thoughts on accommodation and the eating facilities you have seen?

14. Have you ever seen a case of withholding identity documents?

15. Have you seen a factory with an ATM inside the gates?

16. Have you ever wondered why worker interviews rarely yield any particular findings?

17. Did you ever use the bathroom at a factory? What was it like?

18. How would you validate what you have seen?

19. How do you avoid getting sucked into extensive lunches or other delay tactics with factory management?

20. What is the longest time you have spent in – for example – China, Vietnam, or Bangladesh?

21. How often do you travel to visit suppliers, and how long do you usually stay?

22. Have you lived in Asia?

23. What kind of hotel do you normally stay at?

24. What is the breakfast like?

25. What is your preferred means of local transport, and why?

26. What do you think about local taxis?

For questions that receive a positive response, follow up with: 'What did you do then?', 'Who did what?', or, 'How did the factory react?'

For questions that receive a negative response, you can follow up with, 'Why?', or, 'How come?', to make things more open-ended.

What is the rationale behind these questions? Well, the direction of someone's initial education tells something about their natural inclinations. Are they more focused on storytelling (PR), on legalities (law), or practical work (procurement and supply chain)?

Then the practical experience should also be gauged. Depending on their answers, you can gauge how many factories they have in fact attended as anything but a guest of honour. Most Westerners fly in on a

Sunday and depart the following Saturday, spending five working days onsite, visiting two or three sites every day. They will have meetings at several factories, because this indicates higher productivity to their superiors. (Many meetings equals high efficiency … right?)

However, it takes time to understand the lay of the land, and as such two or three meetings per day in different factories allows only very limited understanding and interaction. At the same time, it's very easy for the factory management to clean up in advance, and ensure that any unsightly issues are kept hidden for the duration of the visit. If the visit is short, it's even easier to pretend. As long as the person being impressed doesn't stay too long, short-term appearance is everything.

By asking someone to explain their impression of a factory, you will get an understanding of how they conducted a visit and what they were shown. If they explain it in positive tones, there is a good chance they have only seen the sanitised version, whereas someone with experience will have plenty of good and bad anecdotes to share.

Getting the right person for the right job

Finding the right person for the right job is a must in the same way that you would not want to use a screwdriver as a substitute for a hammer. When I'm asked why this is so important, I often counter with a question similar to, *would you use a butterknife to mow your lawn?* (Of course you wouldn't! Right?)

When seriously sick, you should look for the best doctor, rather than the cheapest doctor … and also not confuse an orthodontist with an ophthalmologist. (They both work with something related to the head, but they are hugely different and the methods used are potentially damaging if used in the wrong place.) I think you get where I am going with this.

It really puzzles me that the market perception for a proficient sustainability professional is almost always by default someone who studied human rights law or PR. While lawyers and PR people may have a particular interest in sustainability and have their 'heart in the right place', presumably they chose their profession based on interest in law or public relations, rather than sustainability or labour conditions in faraway factories in China or other manufacturing hubs in Asia.

Setting the bar like that means that Australian companies miss out because they are not looking in the right places for resources, skills and talent, and the approach and outcome are accordingly poor.

Setting up frameworks and procedures to fit with legislation and communicate what a company intends to do is always worthwhile, but in most other endeavours in business the people who are filling the gap between the frameworks and the communication of the results are also needed. I would compare it with the process of financial reporting where the governance (oversight) aspect is usually signed off by management and the board, and the actual financial report, audited by external auditors, is signed off by the external auditor. But what about the middle? The teams who provide the data that goes into the pack to be audited? The people who gather the data from the different divisions, who ensure that the due diligence process is adequately implemented, and who consolidate the reports that are to be audited?

The missing piece

It seems obvious that there is a piece of the puzzle missing when it comes to practical sustainability, and that there is some education to be done. Maybe this is because sustainability is such a new discipline here in Australia. In placing the responsibility for sustainability with legal or PR/communications, it becomes quite obvious that the company sees it as simply a bolt-on, and while this may seem like a practical solution, it demonstrates that this issue is a lesser priority within the business.

Here is my take on what are the strengths and weaknesses of these different roles related to sustainability:

- A human rights lawyer is very skilled in the principles and legalities of human rights and the legal implications. Human rights lawyers are experts in setting up frameworks and ensuring compliance to the governance piece in the business. Without a doubt, understanding this element is crucial. The weakness comes into play if this person has never seen a real supply chain. After all, you can't have a practical understanding of something you have only studied in a book.

- A PR/communications person is needed to tell the story in a compelling and eloquent manner. At a conference once, I heard a PR person state that telling the story was the most important part, and that 'walk the talk', rightfully should be 'talk the walk'. This kind of statement highlights where many companies are still at: more form over substance. Telling a story eloquently is a skill that easily snares people, but once it's discovered that there is little or no substance, the story itself becomes meaningless and potentially even a liability, because whitewashing and greenwashing have a tendency to come undone when external stakeholders decide to scrutinise what is being boldly claimed.

The missing role between these two functions is the *doer*.

To make sure that stuff gets done, you need someone with supply chain and/or procurement experience. Someone who understand how products move, are manufactured, and sold in real life.

You may be able to ask human rights lawyers or PR professionals to do this work, but ultimately, are they really the right fit? It may be that the corporate legal counsel finds it easier to speak to a human rights lawyer, but consider for a moment what would happen if the chief marketing officer replaced the head of engineering with a marketing person 'because it's easier to communicate' with her ...

Similarly, if the PR professionals are to tell any story at all, someone who has the ability to measure something of substance is crucial to provide documentation for the story being told. Reporting based on anything other than empirical, evidence-based data can quickly be torn apart and expose any well-intentioned efforts as whitewashing.

The sustainable supply chain expert – with a specialist background in bridging both sides of the divide – understands the frameworks, both internally in terms of governance and also externally – that is, the UNGC, the SDGs and so on – and has the experience to tie them together practically, so that they deliver on the goals they were intended to.

So when companies find it overwhelming to respond to the *Modern Slavery Act*, it's probably because they don't have the right understanding of who they need to get the work done in a fulfilling manner, which actually contributes to minimising risk and capturing opportunities.

Wherever the program sits, however the necessary skills are resourced, and whichever way responsibility for the work is parsed out, accountability for any ESG program must be assigned to one person. This is ideally a chief sustainability officer, but it could also sit with the procurement team, legal/general counsel, head of investor relations or the CFO, as long as it is not merely a bolt-on exercise.

IF WORST COMES TO WORST

In the event that an incident occurs and slavery is found in the supply chain or a newspaper exposes poor labour practices at a supplier and the board had no idea, what can we expect then?

If a penalty can be applied (for example, for giving false and misleading statements), mitigating factors may be taken into account and could include:

- self-initiated investigations into incidents, outside of what is required by law and regulations

- a systems and procedures review intended to mitigate future risks of the same type

- remediation measures taken as a result of having a robust emergency plan in place, designed to feed into the review and mitigation process

- proper and documented remediation being carried out

- a rolling due diligence and monitoring plan being in place

- cooperation with the anti-slavery commissioner (in NSW) or the slavery engagement unit in Canberra

- other evidence that the company takes sustainability and slavery seriously.

While the above mitigating factors do not entirely absolve the board of its responsibilities, they will be significant evidence that proper care and due diligence was exercised, to the degree practically possible.

LEGAL TAKE

While I'm not a lawyer, I do note that there are legal opinions whereby the directors' duties are defined in relation to acting diligently to reduce the risk of adverse effects from climate change.[10] It is also noteworthy that the Corporations Act has clear prohibitions on making false and misleading statements.

To me this means that a modern slavery statement must be accurate and clear. To achieve this goal, onsite due diligence must be performed or the directors take the risk that they have not acted to uphold their fiduciary duties.

---

10   See the Hutley Opinion.

6. IMPLEMENTING

Implementation is very company-specific, and depends on the outcomes of the steps in the previous two chapters, Preparing and Defining.

It is not possible to offer company- or industry-specific advice in a book. However, a few pointers to common pitfalls – along with a few things to consider – should provide a good starting point, either for getting underway internally or for hiring a contractor to help develop a plan.

POTENTIAL IMPLEMENTATION PITFALLS

Implementation is where many well-intentioned companies fail, and this is somewhat understandable if the most standard approaches are considered:

- Many companies simply engage their auditors to perform a review of their status. If their auditor has a specialist function in-house, it's often based on only a theoretical understanding of the issues and performed by legal or audit professionals with extensive experience in writing and reviewing procedures and communicating what should be looked into, but little practical experience inside a factory in Asia. This leads to blind spots and miscalculations on what is possible.

• The other issue is that many companies default to an audit or inspection program. This is easy, and can be seen as the element that fills the gap between concepts analysed by the auditors and the practical 'how to' side of things. Auditing is easy, given that most companies already do other types of quality and compliance audits, so the concept is well understood and the process can be easily replicated.

Despite the merits of audits as a tool, there are some significant shortcomings, such as:

– it is costly to engage sufficient capacity to get a full view of the status of the supply chain

– social audits are fundamentally different to quality and other audits, because you can't take partial results at face value; instead, you must consider the entirety of the audit to form an accurate picture of the situation

– the auditor only 'sees' what she is shown, meaning that she can be selective in focus (sometimes this also means that auditor integrity is difficult to maintain)

– the information can be overwhelming, and not aid in the process of improvement.

In my experience, choosing the wrong implementation approach – often as a result of advice given by people without relevant knowledge – leads to only one outcome: no useful results.

To counter this problem, it's advisable to choose someone with real in-factory supply chain experience, not dissimilar to it being preferable to have an orthopaedic surgeon do a hip replacement rather than an orthodontist!

GOOD SUSTAINABLE SUPPLY CHAIN MANAGEMENT

In my experience, good SSCM programs contain these elements:

- monitoring (internal and external)
- active management of risk and issues
- capacity building
- incentives and consequences
- training
- strong vendor relationships
- sharing of best practice
- robust information gathering
- membership of various supporting organisations
- dedicated resources
- external program measurement and evaluation.

Let's look at these issues.

Monitoring should be performed by both internal and external (third party) auditors. Internal auditors are necessary because they have a better understanding of your business and the risks, and this can be used to build stronger relationships as well. External third-party auditors help to isolate responsibility, although there is always a caveat in that the auditor only sees what she is allowed to see.

A good monitoring program will allow active management of risks and issues, and help with feedback to keep the sustainable supply chain strategy updated.

Capacity building is about doing internal and external training and development in regards to the new policies and procedures. And while this is expensive, there are ways to share the costs with other companies. Training of your own team is crucial to ensure that the team is clear on what the policy is and how adherence can have an impact on their jobs and the business.

In this regard, it's also important to ensure that there are incentives and consequences. If a supplier disregards your policy and nothing happens to their status as a supplier, it sends the signal that only lip service needs to be served. Similarly, an incentive scheme to support correct implementation can and should be developed.

Membership of relevant organisations can help with best practice sharing and be a channel for communicating desensitised information with industry peers.

Some organisations also offer databases with shared audit results – such as SEDEX, Amfori, and ETI – which helps to share the burden. The downside to that approach is it also spreads the responsibility, and makes others potentially complicit in any problems.

Another important aspect is resources. Many codes of conduct require dedicated resources from their suppliers to enhance performance, and similarly, any company serious about a sustainable supply chain management program needs a dedicated resource. If a sustainable supply chain manager role is not needed as a full-time position, perhaps consider a part-time person.

Finally, any SSCM program must be measured for reporting purposes. Setting up a robust information-gathering system is necessary. Although many social issues in the supply chain are only measurable by proxy, it is important to try, so that the effort made can be demonstrated.

'It is common sense to take a method and try it. If it fails, admit it frankly and try another. But above all, try something.'

Franklin D. Roosevelt

Get the right help

While it's important to find someone with on-the-ground experience in sustainable supply chain management, it is also useful to have someone who can manage the project integration side of things. Many businesses prefer to find a sustainability subject matter expert who is also qualified to lead the change management, project management and team management aspects of the transformation.

Using outside professional help is also recommended for managing the process of the transition. Only the largest companies maintain a project management office or retain a project management professional as an employee; even fewer maintain a sustainability project manager.

SUSTAINABILITY PROGRAMS AND PROJECTS

While there is often an interchangeable use of 'program' and 'project', there is a technical distinction between the two terms:

- A program contains several projects, and the outputs are defined as benefits. The program benefits can only be realised by coordinating the delivery of several projects.

- A project, on the other hand, delivers project outcomes, as in a product, a service or a specific result. Generally the outcome is a tool or a result.

Undertaking a sustainable supply chain project is usually part of a larger sustainability program, with part elements (projects) related to supply chain, environmental and ecological impact, human rights, impact on society, aiding the UN SDGs, and so on.

However, it is possibly more relevant to look at it as a program, if the desired benefit is to, for example, capture a new client who demands a documented level of sustainability, together with other criteria such as improving lead times, quality, chain of custody and so forth, and where they together form a criteria for supplier selection.

SUSTAINABILITY AS A CHANGE AGENT

The biggest hurdle for many companies is often fully incorporating the new sustainable standards into old practices, procedures and cultures. For the transformation to take full effect, all those aspects must fully embrace the new vision and mission. The good news is that sustainability can be used as a lever to unfreeze other aspects of corporate culture, and reset a new and improved culture, enhanced with sustainable practices.

A skilled sustainability manager can perform aspects of program, project and change management, among others. He will:

- tie the different elements together and manage the progress towards program benefit realisation

- bring clarity to where, within the organisation, changes are necessary

- bring a dedicated and experienced eye to the overarching goal

- focus on developing and attaining a sustainable corporate infrastructure

- clarify the business case for making the transition, based on the focus of each particular department or division

- organise or reorganise the company around sustainable practices and policies, ensuring that all elements are involved and engaged in the process

- ensure that the project outcomes are aiding overall program benefits

- engage stakeholders for maximum impact

- analyse change impact and assess change readiness

- develop a communication plan for how to best convey what is to happen and how it's progressing.

A TEXTILE FACTORY IN HANGZHOU, ZHEJIANG PROVINCE

A factory owner decided that instead of paying salaries to his workers, he would hold the money for them and install an ATM inside the factory compound for the workers to withdraw their money whenever they needed it.

We informed him that this would be non-compliant, especially if he was offering banking services to his staff and had control over how well the ATM was stocked.

Such an arrangement could easily have been misused to underpay the workers, leaving them no remedy to recover their earned wages.

MAPPING SCOPE AND RANGE

When defining your policy, it's a good idea to understand the field in which you are playing. In sporting terms, you may decide if you are going to play defence or offence, or somewhere in between. You may also want to define if you are going to match your competitor's strategy or look for areas where their defences are weak.

In order to understand the lay of the land, you can benchmark your competition and then map out your own ambitions relative to that. This will allow you to establish how you want to configure your own approach measured across policies, processes, monitoring programs, resources, reporting and so forth.

By mapping it out as shown below, you gain clear visibility of your competitors, their approach and their ESG score. This will help you define your targets.

Competitor positioning mapping

	Bare minimum	Average approach	Best practice
Human rights policy	Us	–	Competitor X
SAQ	–	Competitor X/ Us	–
Due diligence	–	Us	Competitor X
Monitoring	–	Us	Competitor X
Compliance	Us	Competitor X	–
Conformance	–	Competitor X/ Us	–
Etc.	Us	–	Competitor X
ESG scores	Competitor X: 80/100		Us: 65/100

The next step is to extend this mapping with an overlay of your strategy, to understand where your gaps are and define how to fill the gaps and/or expand on the areas you see as a strategic strength.

It is also worthwhile aligning your general risk management framework to the gaps identified, and understanding how you can increase the proportion of managed risk versus unmanaged risks.

THE MATERIALITY PROCESS

Materiality is more than the traditional equity approach to what is important. It looks beyond equity and ownership, and it is used to identify and establish priorities for what constitute significant risks and opportunities for improvements related to environmental, social and governance (ESG), as well as economic factors as seen from the business and from the perspective of its key stakeholders.

A thorough materiality process is at the core of efficient strategic decision-making, and it guides the strategic response to achieve either mitigation of risks or realisation of opportunities. It establishes importance relative to stakeholders as well as their impact on the entity, and it aids in determining the priority of issues.

If done correctly, the materiality process is an important aid to filter or funnel the myriad issues that could influence the business and its operations. It also demonstrates good governance to – in particular – external stakeholders; that is, investors.

When starting out, it's easy to find hundreds of issues, but that does not mean that each is of importance or even merits attention.

The process to arrive at the material issues can be either thorough and deep and done with an impeccable, methodological approach (a top-shelf approach) *or* less scientifically rigorous.

Many large consultancies have developed a cookie-cutter approach, where material is lost and results become quite standardised. Carrying out a top-shelf materiality process is expensive, and if you can accept the trade-off, the cookie-cutter approach may be sufficient to – at least – not be left behind by the competition.

What is also important to consider is that the materiality process should take an approach not just defined by equity ownership in an asset or organisation. It must also include stakeholders that are external, and outside the traditional sphere of direct influence merited by ownership.

Best practice prescribes that:

1. Steps taken to identify, prioritise and validate material issues are described.

2. Stakeholder mapping is performed and actively put to use.

3. Societal trends are evaluated for their: ability to influence desired outcomes; probability and impact; risk mitigation needs; and allowing proper countermeasures to be implemented to cushion the business entity from adverse consequences.

4. Material issues are publicly disclosed in a format that highlights an order of priority.

5. If appropriate, the process should include and recognise differences between geographies, business units and product categories.

6. The process should align to the sustainability report, including ensuring that the strategy addresses the issues, targets and KPIs.

7. The process should provide documented evidence of mitigating activities, application, and controls applied to measure the outcome.

8. The process should demonstrate validation of the results of the materiality analysis.

In practical (simplified) terms, the process could start by taking these steps:

1. Brainstorm issues that could be of importance.

2. Engage stakeholders to identify additional issues, and to validate issues from the initial cut.

3. Rank and rate.

4. Prioritise working with the top issues.

The ranking and prioritisation of issues to be dealt with is very important as it underlines the efforts required to achieve the desired outcomes.

Before engaging in the actual ranking, it is a good idea to understand the stakeholder power positions and their relative interest in the topic at hand. To do this, Mendelow's stakeholder management matrix is a useful tool. It allows you to weight the issues based on where they originate. This is not to say that issues originating in the low power/low interest quadrant should be disregarded – especially given that issues can be shared across stakeholder groups. The origin of the issue is of value to weighting the importance and feasibility of including it in the select group of material issues to be worked on.

Mendelow's stakeholder management matrix

Stakeholder power	**High**	**Keep satisfied** (Make sure not to disregard or disengage stakeholders in this category)	**Key player** (Disregard a key player at your own peril!)
	Low	**Minimal effort** (Any stakeholder is important, if mapped, but be realistic as to their potential impact on the issue. Pretty clear, right?)	**Keep informed** (Keep informed, but don't spend too much time here)
		Low	**High**

Stakeholder interest

Adapted from Mendelow's Stakeholder Management Matrix

Once your stakeholder mapping is done, you can proceed to make a hot-spot map of the material issues identified with the stakeholders.

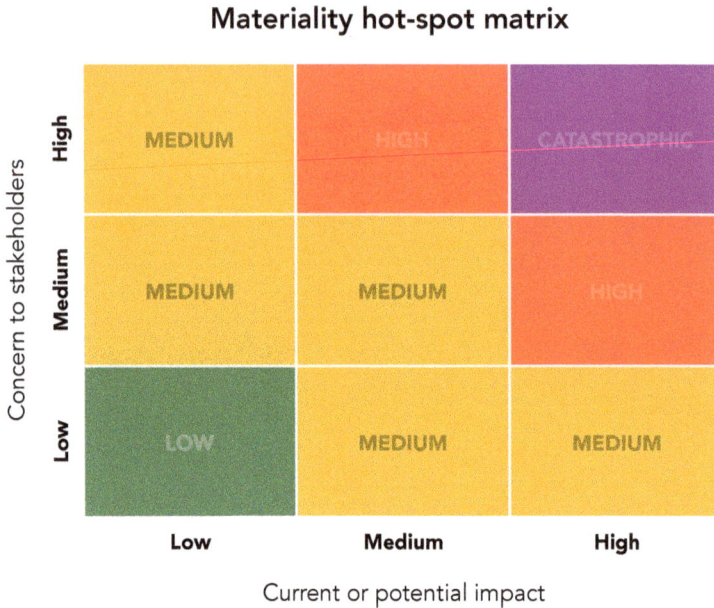

Materiality hot-spot matrix

Concern to stakeholders			
High	MEDIUM	HIGH	CATASTROPHIC
Medium	MEDIUM	MEDIUM	HIGH
Low	LOW	MEDIUM	MEDIUM
	Low	Medium	High

Current or potential impact

At the end of the process, the outcome should provide an overview of what items are absolutely critical to address; that is, having both high current or potential impact as well as high concern to the stakeholders involved.

This is different to a traditional risk management framework where the axis illustrating the concern to stakeholders is replaced with a probability rating rather than a concern (or interest) rating. In any case, something with a potential high impact on the business must be addressed.

Establishing what is material allows you to address what is important, rather than focusing on irrelevant distractions.

TRAINING AND DEVELOPMENT

Training is a key aspect of any change management, and for something that is not a minor change to the way business is conducted, extra efforts are required. It is easy to underestimate how much training and L&D effort is needed to effectively get the organisation on the same page.

The capacity needed depends on the level of application you settle on. If you are aiming for the bare minimum, a simple compliance training may suffice. On the other hand, if you are working towards a major organisational change initiative, where you are not only aiming to change a few procedural aspects, but also culture (hearts and minds), then something more substantial is desirable to properly anchor the change in the organisation.

Any training program should start with creating a gap analysis of where the team is at and where the desired end point is. If a wider organisational change effort is taking place and if you are attempting to utilise this process as a lever for general change, then a more comprehensive change management approach is necessary.

Depending on the outcome of the gap analysis, you can then develop the actual training.

Key considerations:

- Should it be training delivered at the time of the policies coming into force?

- Should it be part of ongoing training for compliance purposes?

- How long should it be?

    - One slide in a general new staff induction?

    - Full-day training once a year?

    - Or some other format ...

- Who is the target audience?
  - Internal:
    - ~ broad focus
    - ~ narrow focus.
  - External:
    - ~ suppliers
    - ~ management
    - ~ staff (workers)
    - ~ agents, intermediaries, etc.
  - Personalities and learning styles?
- Who is to deliver the training?
  - Internal subject matter experts?
  - External experts?
  - Train-the-trainer?
  - Other?
- Can it be delivered via an electronic platform, as part of general compliance training?
- Can it be combined with anti-money laundering and anti-bribery and corruption trainings?

There are many places to find inspiration for the training. The Danish Institute of Human Rights makes many training resources freely available. Nestlé also has made their training (developed with The Danish Institute of Human Rights) available free of charge. Anti-Slavery Australia also has training materials available, as do Walk Free and many others.

Training is necessary for your team to understand what they are expected to do, and why. Perhaps the 'why' is even more important than the 'what', because if they understand why they are doing what you ask, they will naturally seek out the 'what' and it is much more likely to be done.

While implementing training is normally the task of human resources, it's important that it is developed in collaboration with the departments that are more affected on a day-to-day basis, to align with general processes of operations and also to aid the anchoring into the general culture of doing business.

Conscious Competence Learning Model

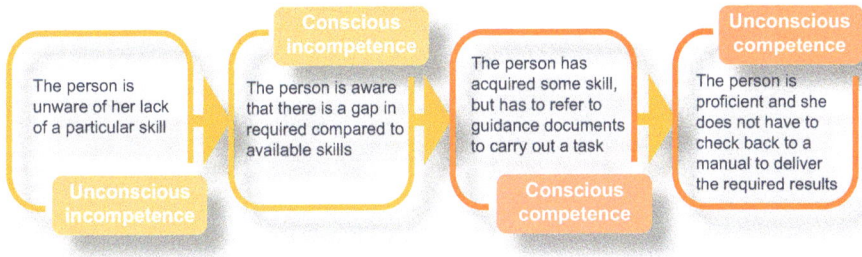

Unconscious incompetence	Conscious incompetence	Conscious competence	Unconscious competence
The person is unware of her lack of a particular skill	The person is aware that there is a gap in required compared to available skills	The person has acquired some skill, but has to refer to guidance documents to carry out a task	The person is proficient and she does not have to check back to a manual to deliver the required results

The desire is to bring people on the journey from unconscious incompetence to conscious incompetence, through to conscious competence, and arrive at unconscious competence, where the awareness is automatic.

To move the team from the unconscious incompetence stage to unconscious competence, mapping the team's skills is invaluable. To perform such a mapping, a KSA chart (**K**nowledge, **S**kills, **A**ttitudes) can be used to understand the strengths and gaps of the team and map out what modules needs to be developed and deployed to meet the requirements.

KSA chart

Activity	Knowledge	Skills	Attitudes
Due diligence	What are the steps? What process is applied? How to control the outcome?	Assessing Setting up new due diligence account Relationships Asking non-direct questions	Vigilant Astute Care for the outcome
Audit coordination	Understand the standards against which to audit	Etc.	Etc.
Etc.	Etc.	Etc.	Etc.

Adapted from *The Effective Change Manager's Handbook.*

Once you have the KSA chart, you can start assessing what is required to bring the team up to the desired standard.

If the team is large, or different KSA profiles are needed, the next step is to rate and rank who needs to know more; that is, nice to have, who it is important to, and for whom it is business-critical to be fully trained and informed.

This mapping will also help to establish the learning method to be applied. In broad terms, the learning methods are:

- one to one

- small group

- group lecture
- workshops and interactive learning
- large presentations
- formal courses
- computer-aided training
- computer simulations
- practical simulations
- on-the job training (simulation of real cases).

In my personal experience, a combination of on-the job training, interactive presentations and workshops mixed with interactive learning can be very helpful, but at the end of the day, everyone has different learning styles, so ideally it should be applied according to individual needs and with an eye on budgets and resources available.

7. MONITORING AND EVALUATING

Achieving any goal will require a collaborative approach between key stakeholders as well as an approach containing several elements, tools and measuring points. Setting out on the sustainable supply chain project, it's important to ensure that it is appropriately targeted and completed as efficiently as possible. That means getting clear on what is to be achieved, by when, and using only the necessary effort. (In the previous chapter we saw the elements that should be included in a sustainable supply chain management program.)

However, it is not always feasible to have an extensive sustainable supply chain management program in place by comprehensively implementing all of the required elements from the outset. You can choose a scalable solution or plan for implementing additional depth of process steps as you progress. This can be either in a planned fashion or an ad hoc 'cross the bridge when we get there' approach.

In this chapter we will examine the various monitoring and evaluation issues you must be aware of to successfully implement your program.

THE MINIMUM APPROACH

It is advisable to understand what the minimum requirements are, which will allow you to start reporting with a degree of confidence. The bare minimum program of works consists of the following components, and revolves around screening for social and labour risks:

- risk assessment:

  - a negative list

  - SAQ

- supplier due diligence

- supplier monitoring.

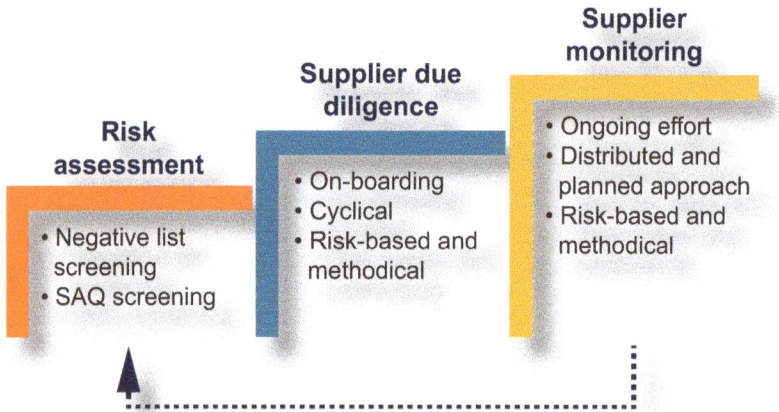

In combination, these three components will enable pre-screening of supplier risks and provide a basis for ongoing performance evaluation and reporting.

The methodology should ensure that:

- you have tools used for screening that suppliers align with your risk-management framework

- suppliers are appropriately screened for social and labour risks, prior to on-boarding

- suppliers are continually monitored for social and labour risk performance

- a consistent documentation system is in place, to feed into your company's overall risk-management and reporting frameworks.

SUPPLIER RISK ASSESSMENTS

Both elements of the initial risk-assessment component should be developed to filter potential suppliers according to a set of predefined criteria, using a negative-list approach. This will allow a refinement of the supplier candidate field, which can then proceed into a pathway of increasingly detailed sets of questions, ending with either elimination or in a predefined due diligence process.

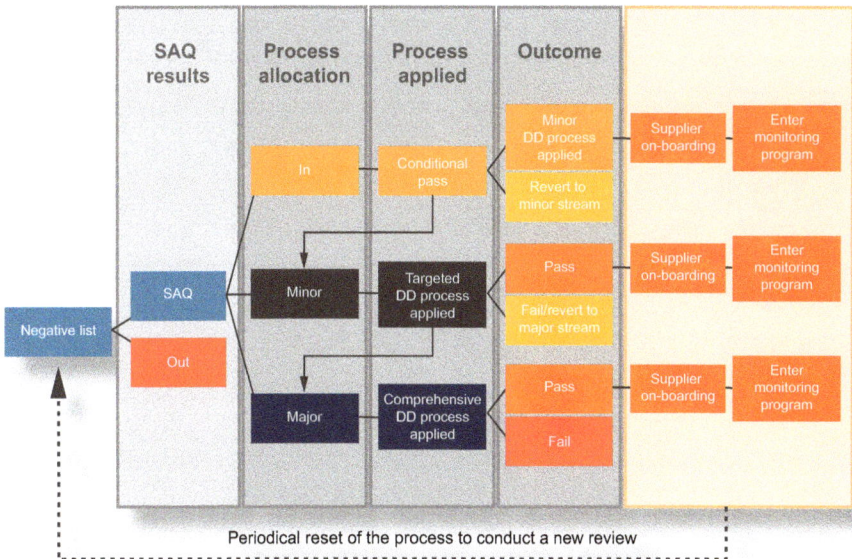

Periodical reset of the process to conduct a new review

The process must be designed to establish where more information must be obtained to proceed, or alternatively end the process (that is, disengage from a supplier).

Negative lists

The purpose of a negative list is to enable vetting of long-listed suppliers against non-compatible criteria and your values. While a negative list is not part of the process mentioned above, it is the simplest form of screening available.

Negative screening could include parameters such as:

- certain industries (such as gambling, tobacco and munitions)

- geography (such as high-risk countries, such as North Korea, Uzbekistan and Pakistan)

- capacity and quality

- ability to disclose certain types of information

- absence of certain policies or procedures

- presence of criminal rulings, ongoing legal proceedings and the like.

While negative screening isn't new to procurement, the application of it with the aim of achieving a sustainable supply chain is somewhat more of a novelty. Investors are also increasingly applying positive and negative screening filters to evaluate and justify investment decisions.

A negative list is normally expressly stated in a policy or a guidance; for example, in the following form: 'We will not engage in sourcing activities from North Korea', or, 'We will not invest in companies associated with gambling'.

A negative screening filter can be the first step of the process that will allow companies to either enter or remain as part of the active suppliers database.

Self-assessment questionnaires

A self-assessment questionnaire (SAQ) should be the first step in reviewing a potential supplier, and it is a step to establish the initial risk profile of that supplier.

The outcome of the SAQ could lead to a defined due diligence path for the supplier vying for your orders, or alternatively it could lead to the supplier being excluded from further tendering opportunities and being exited from the supplier pool, or at the very least placed in quarantine until improvements are implemented and properly documented.

An SAQ should never be considered the end of the process, and answers to it should always be backed up with evidence. Some key considerations regarding effective SAQ designs are:

- There will most likely be misinterpretations and misunderstandings about how the questions should be answered.

- Any SAQ should be crafted with careful reference to applicable legislation, guidelines and standards.

- A questionnaire can never fully represent the real situation at the supplier.

- Prior to drafting the questions, you should take care to confirm and understand your code of conduct (if this exists), values and desired outcomes.

- Questions should always allow for attaching documentary evidence.

Key areas to be covered are:

- organisational governance

- accountability and responsibility

- management systems

- human rights

- modern slavery

- social and labour and conditions

- environment

- stakeholder engagement

- grievance and remediation procedures

- probity

- subcontracting.

The process can be divided into several stages as a filtering or funnelling mechanism, providing gateways or access points to the next level, but the key is to strike the right balance. I have seen companies settle on 10 questions and others settle on 250. The variation is large, but the key issue to keep in mind is the purpose and how much it is intended to overlap with the due diligence process, which comes after the SAQ and the risk assessment coming out of it.

The questions should allow you to establish sufficient data points to triangulate the likeliness of errors and falsifications. They also shouldn't use too direct nor ambiguous language. Examples of questions that may be counterproductive are:

- Do you pay minimum legal wages?

- Do you intend to hire any more child labourers?

While these questions may seem a bit farfetched, I have seen questions to that effect before.

Some better questions would look like this:

Where do your workers come from?			
☐ Vietnam	☐ Indonesia	☐ Taiwan	☐ Other

If the factory is located in Taiwan but 95% of the workers come from Vietnam and Indonesia, that is a red flag for potential labour exploitation, and something that should be used to define the due diligence pathway.

Another example of a poorly designed question could be:

- Do you prevent the workers from leaving the premises?

- Do the workers need permission to leave?

The answer to such a question can only try to hide the true facts. Instead, ask questions such as:

Where do your workers live while they work for you?		
☐ Dormitories	☐ Self-arranged accommodation off the factory site	☐ Other

If the majority live in dormitories (and they can be quite grubby), there is an indicator that should be looked into.

That question is then expanded on later with a question like:

When do you open/close the factory gate for free passage?		
☐ Morning	☐ Lunch break	☐ Evening
☐ Never – If never, specify why.		

You can start gauging how the workers move around, if they are restricted, and if they are exploited; for example, by being asked to pay above market rate for compulsory housing.

Developing a comprehensive self-assessment questionnaire takes time and experience, not only in wordsmithing the questions but also onsite in the factories.

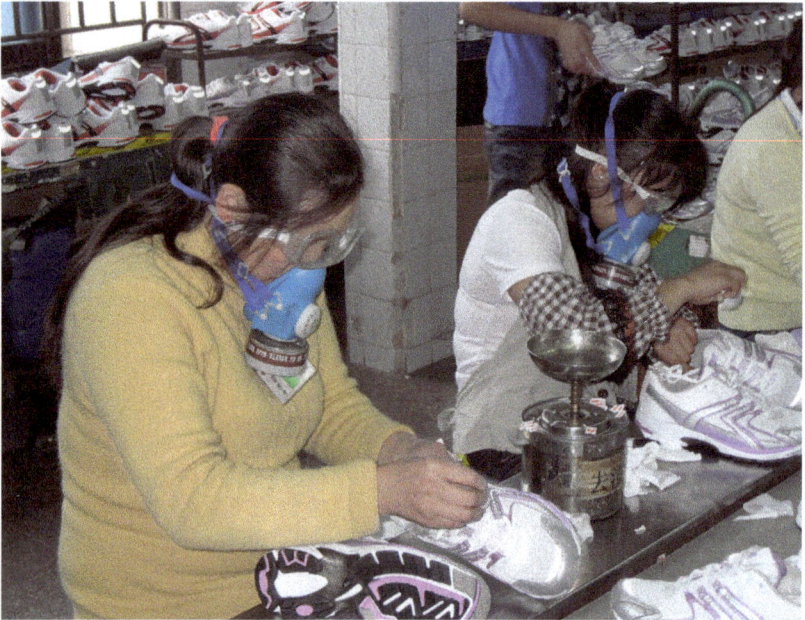

Consider for a moment a situation I found in China, where the factory was providing PPE for the audit day. An inattentive auditor could easily have overlooked that the lady shown was wearing her eye protection upside down and that the mask wasn't fitted properly to prevent her inhaling glue vapours.

The supplier would have ticked 'Yes' in the box asking if proper PPE was worn, and if this had only been a desktop review by an inexperienced consultant, this important issue would have gone unnoticed, and remained a liability.

Questions should never be Yes/No, alone. Instead, evidence must be provided to help form an opinion on the accuracy of any claim or answer.

And again, while an SAQ requests honest answers, the answers are most often interpreted by the person answering, either because they do not know the right answer or, in the worst of cases, because they do not want to limit their options with a negative answer.

Therefore, any completed SAQ must be read with caution (take it with a grain of salt), and individual answers should be used to calibrate the overall truthfulness of the SAQ answers. It is after all only a pointer to what to look further into in the subsequent steps.

As a small cautionary point, I would also advise you to be vigilant in regards to the development of the SAQ, as to whose benefit it serves. Because of the ambiguity of the responses, the same point can be made about the questions, and if for example you let your audit supplier help you formulate the SAQ, the questions it contains may subtly play into getting metrics that warrant additional audits. This skewing of the outcome may not necessarily come from a self-serving position, but it is something you should be aware of. The purpose of the SAQ is to flag the correct number of suppliers for audit, not to fill the coffers of your third-party auditor.

SUPPLIER DUE DILIGENCE

Due diligence should focus on validating if a supplier is likely to be capable of delivering the outcome it is contracted to deliver and on the agreed terms. It should also establish further actions to be undertaken to maintain the risk profile at an acceptable level.

These further actions are to establish a framework for when and what elements a supplier social due diligence should include, and it will largely depend on the outcome of the SAQ, follow-up requests for additional documentation in combination with category risk profiles, and geographical risks.

To establish a baseline against which to measure progress, a scoring mechanism must be established. This mechanism will also act as an objective filter for when and what level of social due diligence is to be performed on a supplier candidate.

The mechanism will determine the risk of harm by judging the supplier candidates on a scale (the gravity of adverse impacts) and scope.

The scoring matrix should also consider:

- whether the candidate will be a direct or indirect supplier of the final products

- the level of existing compliance

- the extent of information provided (including provision of evidence for each question)

- the veracity of information (the ability to validate the responses)

- the track record of each candidate.

It is also advisable for the due diligence risk framework to establish decision gateways where, in the case of negative findings, the monitoring process (component three of the framework) should revert to a due diligence process.

The Due Diligence Risk Framework is to be used to establish a baseline for each supplier, against which performance can be measured. The outcome of the Due Diligence Risk Framework will enable a qualitative assessment on the degree of scrutiny to be applied to supplier candidates prior to on-boarding.

SUPPLIER MONITORING PROGRAMS

The supplier monitoring component will establish a 'who–what–where–when–what if' framework for monitoring as part of business as usual (BaU).

The monitoring framework would usually contain the following elements:

- generic risk monitoring (category and geographic)

- individual supplier monitoring

- a corrective actions program

- when to revert to due diligence.

The monitoring program should be aligned with the due diligence program, to allow for KPI tracking and reporting (for a slavery statement and/or the company's sustainability report).

It is common to develop a rolling monitoring plan, deployed in phases and taking overall risk parameters into account, as shown below.

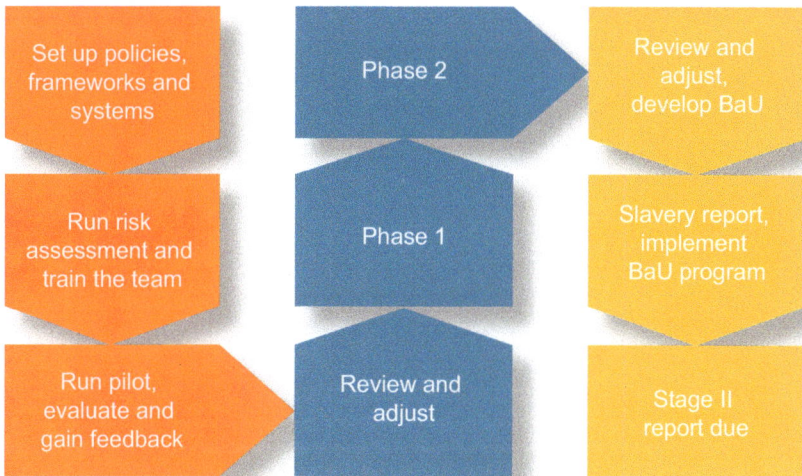

Set up policies, frameworks and systems	Phase 2	Review and adjust, develop BaU
Run risk assessment and train the team	Phase 1	Slavery report, implement BaU program
Run pilot, evaluate and gain feedback	Review and adjust	Stage II report due

It is advisable that the monitoring framework defines which, and to what extent, third-party auditors are to be used, if and how internal team members should conduct 'audit-like' inspections (second-party audit), and timeframes for when to look into what.

A corrective actions program is a key element to any monitoring program to deal with findings from the monitoring process. This is dealt with further below.

Finally, the monitoring program will establish criteria for when to revert to due diligence.

A well-defined and developed supplier monitoring program will ensure social monitoring efforts are applied efficiently and consistently, according to predefined criteria and as part of BaU. It will help manage risks, and establish documentation for the ongoing purpose of risk and reputational management, as well as provide backstopping in case blame is cast on your business for not doing enough.

IN-COUNTRY VETTING

It is my experience that third-party audits are not the most effective means of supplier screening. While third-party auditors often follow a well-developed procedure, they will still only see what is being shown to them. Their perspective is also always different to yours, and hence their understanding of your risks is – at best – representative, yet never fully aligned.

For practical reasons, businesses often outsource part of the in-country vetting program, but it is good to have an internal function allowing internal teams an opportunity to calibrate the findings on site.

CORRECTIVE ACTIONS PLANS

A corrective actions program (also called remediation) is a key element to any monitoring program to deal with findings from the monitoring process.

Monitoring as part of BaU will find and review changes to previous findings, but it is also important to have a corrective actions management system in place. This could be following up on findings; for example, asking the supplier to send documentary evidence via email or file transfer to ensure that agreed corrective actions have in fact been addressed. In my experience, we would ask suppliers to take photos of the visible improvements onsite at the manufacturer (for example, installing safety equipment), and send through policies and written documentation in written format for us to review and assess.

Having a methodology to ensure corrective actions have been properly implemented is important. After all, if the same issues persist, the problem may be underlying, and the issues in the Corrective Action Plan may be merely symptoms of poor governance.

SUPPLY CHAIN COMPLIANCE VERSUS SUPPLY CHAIN CONFORMANCE

'Compliance' and 'conformance' are often used interchangeably, but there is a difference. 'Compliance' is a legal term. 'Conformance' is usually not legally binding, and is used to describe adherence to standards.

While the difference may seem semantic, it is more than that; for example, in the automotive industry, a car must comply with the regulations to be allowed to drive on the road. Compliance is part of the vehicle approval. Manufacturers will also do conformity of production (CoP) assessments at predefined intervals.

In some cases the conformity of production is a legal requirement for continued compliance. But in other cases it is at the business's discretion, and yet they still decide to undertake extensive CoP programs because it secures documentation that the product is manufactured under the correct standards and hence continues to live up to the compliance requirements as set out at the initial approval process.

Running an efficient CoP will help safeguard the business against claims it acted without proper due care and diligence, in case of accusations that it didn't.

TECHNOLOGY AND SSCM

The key to any good sustainable supply chain management system is to have solid data collection processes in place, and ensuring that the data is not corrupted. After all, at the end of the day, reporting on progress and efficiency of the measures taken can only be done if there is good data. Apart from information from audit reports, your own site visits and other external due diligence processes (which is the standard level of information available today), the future is offering some exciting new opportunities to collect additional data, and/or triangulate it with other information sources.

Wearables

I am not talking about Fitbits or Apple watches – at least, not yet. I am talking about cameras with the ability to livestream a site visit over the internet.

While the technology might not be at a point where this option is seamless and second best to being there in person, it is evolving. Several action camera manufacturers have versions out which are supposed to be able to livestream, and several are marketing 180-degree or 360-degree camera systems.

Once it becomes possible to livestream reliably and remotely, ask an auditor to perform tasks or look into things the viewer has spotted, as it becomes difficult to hide issues.

For it to be a reliable option, it requires a good mobile connection that is not interfered with by various national firewalls and other scrubbing mechanisms. It also requires geo-location verification via GPS, and finally auditors who are willing to take orders from inspectors far away.

In the future, such devices may even assist in translation of paperwork found onsite – similar to what we already see with Google Translate's camera function, where you can point it at a sign and get a reading of what it means in your chosen language.

Risk management software

There are many options for compiling information and scoring it according to external and internal parameters.

Generally the solutions that are better at this job draw on large datasets, rather than internal information sources. For example, EcoVadis, which has insights into entire industries across different factors. Other good examples are BSI VerifEye, Verisk Maplecroft, SAP Ariba, Control Risks, FRDM, Transparency-One and Avetta.

The strongest solutions depend on the ability to accurately assess your risk, as well as their ability to analyse and report on the overall performance for the sustainability report and the Modern Slavery Report.

Block chain

While block chain offers some promise – for storing contracts, and perhaps for ensuring payments reach their intended recipients in the amounts agreed – there are to my mind still plenty of questions to be asked in regards to this.

As for all other systems, what is paramount is that the inputs are of quality. Garbage in equals garbage out, and as long as we are dealing with humans, there are ways around how it will work versus how it was intended to work.

As a standalone solution it is not sufficient, but as a complementary technology, ways will be found to utilise this technology well to support the Sustainable Supply Chain Management efforts.

Artificial intelligence

This is probably the most interesting tech element. Having been involved in a project where we analysed audit reports for trends and patterns, it was evident how artificial intelligence can be very useful. Prior to that particular project, the audit organisation had to manually filter data, and a team member had to do a manual investigation. This was time intensive and resources were limited. As such, it was like looking for the proverbial needle in a haystack. But utilising pattern recognition technology and finetuning it along the way enabled a narrowing of the team's focus to areas where the analysis showed there was reason to look.

Once algorithms are finetuned even more, they may even be used to scan facial expressions of workers during interviews to understand if the worker is under duress, has been coached to answer according to a predefined manual, or is otherwise not telling the truth. This – in combination with experienced auditors, livestreaming and block chain – will greatly improve the ability to understand what is the true situation at the site being visited.

THE IMPACT OF SCOPE AND ASSUMPTIONS

When developing the SSCM, the scope and assumptions are highly influential as to what the system will be designed to measure (efficiently). The following points should be considered when developing the SSCM process methodology:

- The scope must cover risks related to social factors; that is, labour conditions, modern slavery, and adherence to the business's social code of conduct.

- It should fit into the procurement process without providing excessive overlaps – it should not replace it.

- Measurables at each end-point should feed into the next, without creating misaligned data sets.

- Supplier analysis, risk assessment and due diligence methodology should be focused on supplier selection and on-boarding, while monitoring relates to the ongoing efforts to manage supplier social and labour risks.

- A review of policies related to bribery, anti-corruption, money laundering and environmental sustainability should be considered to ensure they align and support the SSCM efforts.

- How large a proportion of the work can be delivered as desk work versus how much must be done onsite.

- Are workshops with stakeholders (internally and externally) necessary or a prerequisite for success?
- Are training sessions necessary for general embedding into the organisation and the supplier base?

Scoping any project correctly from the outset is of vital importance to ensure that it is adequately resourced and that stakeholder expectations are aligned.

8. THE MODERN SLAVERY ACTS

At the time of writing, Australia has two modern slavery legislations: the Commonwealth and the NSW legislation. The Commonwealth legislation passed parliament *after* the NSW legislation, yet it was assented to *before* the NSW legislation. Despite the NSW *Modern Slavery Act* having received assent and being due to come into force on 1 July 2019, at the time of writing it has been sent back to the NSW Legislative Council Standing Committee on Social Issues, due to inconsistencies between the two pieces of legislation. It is a so-called Section 109 inconsistency, which refers to the Australian constitution, where Section 109 states that in case of inconsistencies, the Commonwealth legislation takes precedence. In other words, Commonwealth legislation overrules state legislation. Time will tell when and if the Act will come into force, but at the moment it is uncertain what will happen.

The Australian Commonwealth legislation was enacted on 1 January 2019, and the first reporting period runs from 1 July 2019 to 30 June 2020. This means that the first deadline for submitting the modern slavery statement is 31 December 2020. The word is that the NSW legislation timings will be aligned with the Commonwealth legislation.

WHAT ARE THE MODERN SLAVERY ACTS?

Plenty has been written and said about the Acts (both the Commonwealth and the NSW Act), so I will spare you many of the details. Chances are that if you are reading this book, you have probably attended one of the many *Modern Slavery Act* 'conferences', essentially regurgitating the same information over and over, but to a large degree the same 'experts'.

Chances are also that you already knew slavery was illegal prior to the *Modern Slavery Act* coming into force, but that enforcement was hard, because there simply weren't sufficient resources put into understanding far-away supply chains, or for that matter seeing what often was right under our noses in small takeaway outlets and franchise businesses: exploited and often underpaid workers.

The biggest change from the previous regime is that the board of directors are to sign and submit a modern slavery statement, and they must be well informed to actually sign. Slavery is illegal; now part of the responsibility for this can be placed on the shoulders – if no more than morally – of those supposed to inform themselves of any situations in the supply chain, namely the board of directors.

KEY DIFFERENCES BETWEEN THE ACTS

While the Commonwealth and NSW Acts are very similar, they do have some significant differences. The Commonwealth legislation has 'less teeth' than its NSW counterpart, most notably:

- It has no anti-slavery commissioner.

- It has no penalties for non-compliance (reporting according to the mandatory requirements).

- The reporting threshold is $100,000 million (double the amount for the NSW legislation).

Requirements	NSW *Modern Slavery Act*	Commonwealth *Modern Slavery Act*
Revenue threshold	$50M – $100M	$100M
Penalties for non-compliance	Up to: $1.1M for failure to prepare a statement $1.1M for failure to publish a statement $1.1M for providing false or misleading information	Option to 'name and shame'
Anti-slavery commissioner	Yes	No
Body overseeing reporting	Independent Anti-slavery Commissioner	Business Engagement Unit/ Modern Slavery Engagement Unit
Pathway to voluntary reporting	No/To be determined	Yes
Commencement	To be determined	1 January 2019

One of the possible inconsistencies is that companies can report voluntarily, which creates a possible loophole where companies who fall within the NSW legislation's threshold ($50 million turnover) can opt to report according to the Commonwealth legislation. Then they can submit a substandard report which under NSW legislation would merit a penalty, but under the Commonwealth legislation is penalty free.

Another key issue is there is no pathway to voluntary reporting in the NSW legislation, which could be a problem for companies that oscillate around the threshold.

SEVEN MANDATORY CRITERIA

Companies that must report must address seven mandatory criteria covering:

1. the reporting entity

2. structure, operations and supply chain mapping

3. risks of modern slavery

4. steps taken to assess and address the risks

5. how effective the steps taken are at addressing modern slavery risks

6. the internal consultation

7. any other relevant information.

The statement, under the Commonwealth legislation, must be submitted to the Department of Home Affairs–run central registry, from where it will be publicly available.

Following the steps outlined in this book will allow you to report according to these seven criteria. However, it will also equip you to populate your non-financial and sustainability report on areas surrounding and often leading to modern slavery.

In my view, a key point is that if you do not go to see the supplier's facilities with your own eyes, you are not in a position to effectively address Criteria 3, 4 and 5, and therefore you cannot report in a trustworthy manner.

RISK RESPONSE

When addressing slavery risks, it's important to consider that the response should be proportionate to your business's involvement. The Commonwealth *Modern Slavery Act 2018* Guidance for Reporting Entities references the UN Guiding Principles, Principle 19:[11]

In order to prevent and mitigate adverse human rights impacts, business enterprises should integrate the findings from their impact assessments across relevant internal functions and processes, and take appropriate action.

(a) Effective integration requires that:

  (i) Responsibility for addressing such impacts is assigned to the appropriate level and function within the business enterprise;

  (ii) Internal decision-making, budget allocations and oversight processes enable effective responses to such impacts.

(b) Appropriate action will vary according to:

  (i) Whether the business enterprise causes or contributes to an adverse impact, or whether it is involved solely because the impact is directly linked to its operations, products or services by a business relationship;

  (ii) The extent of its leverage in addressing the adverse impact.

Source: UN Guiding Principles, Principle 19

---

11 Guiding Principles on Business and Human Rights, Implementing the United Nations 'Protect, Respect and Remedy' Framework.

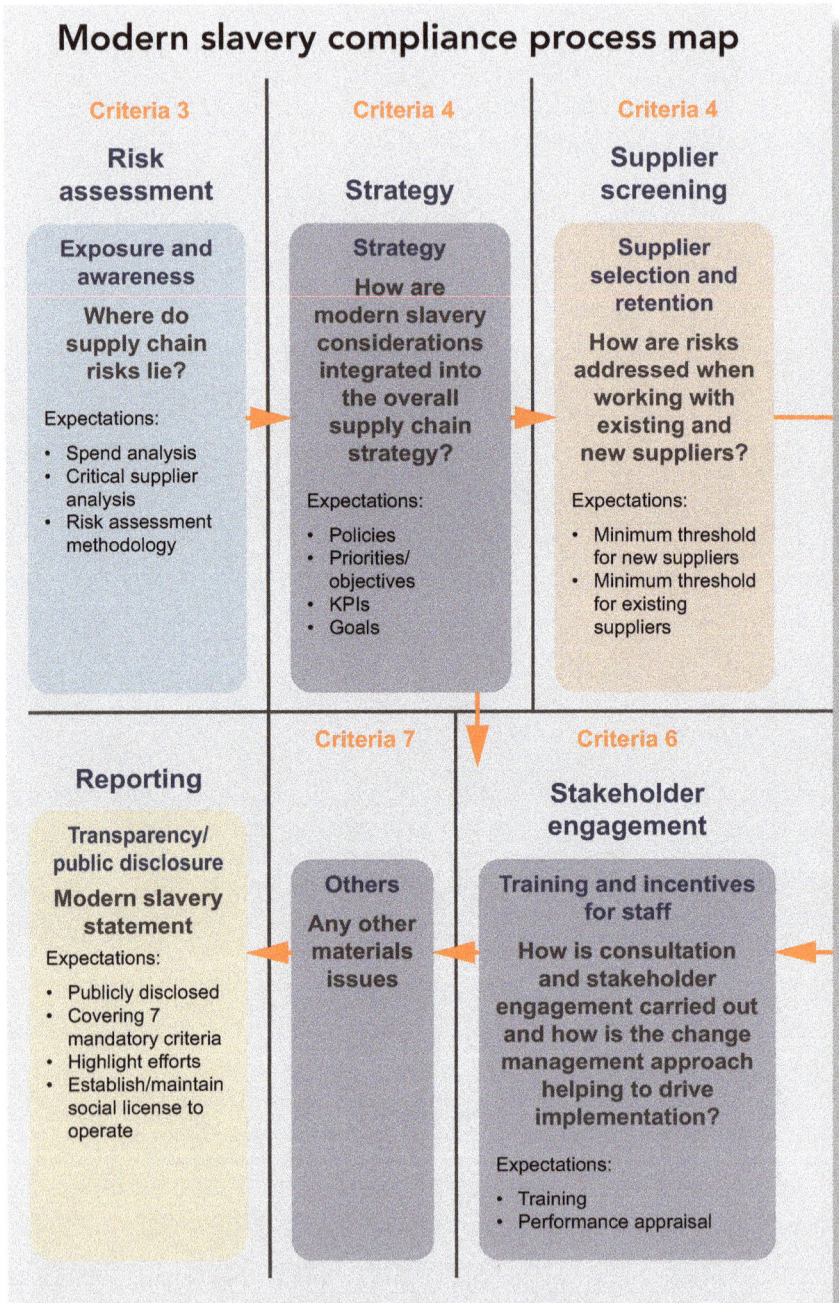

Modern slavery compliance process map

Criteria 3

Risk assessment

Exposure and awareness

Where do supply chain risks lie?

Expectations:
- Spend analysis
- Critical supplier analysis
- Risk assessment methodology

Criteria 4

Strategy

Strategy

How are modern slavery considerations integrated into the overall supply chain strategy?

Expectations:
- Policies
- Priorities/ objectives
- KPIs
- Goals

Criteria 4

Supplier screening

Supplier selection and retention

How are risks addressed when working with existing and new suppliers?

Expectations:
- Minimum threshold for new suppliers
- Minimum threshold for existing suppliers

Reporting

Transparency/ public disclosure

Modern slavery statement

Expectations:
- Publicly disclosed
- Covering 7 mandatory criteria
- Highlight efforts
- Establish/maintain social license to operate

Criteria 7

Others

Any other materials issues

Criteria 6

Stakeholder engagement

Training and incentives for staff

How is consultation and stakeholder engagement carried out and how is the change management approach helping to drive implementation?

Expectations:
- Training
- Performance appraisal

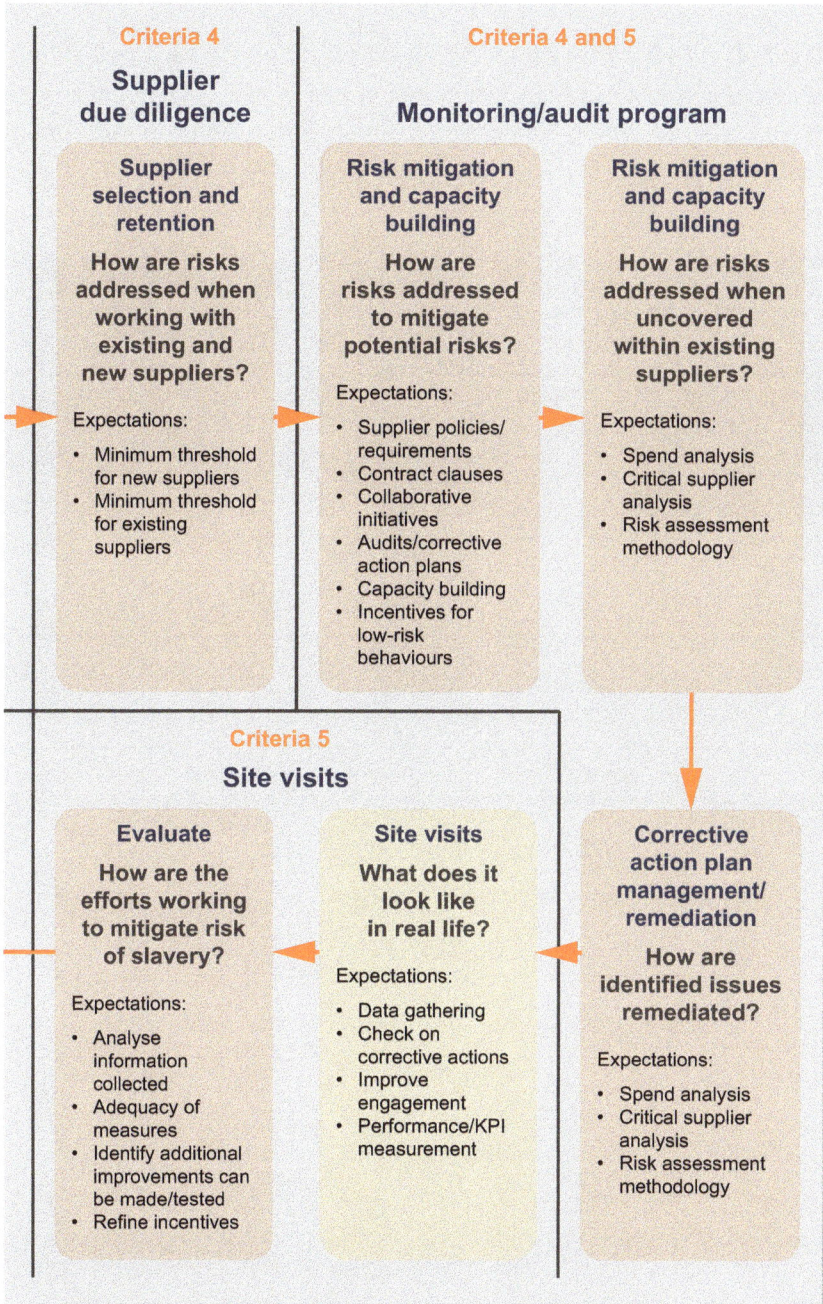

Criteria 4

Supplier due diligence

Supplier selection and retention

How are risks addressed when working with existing and new suppliers?

Expectations:

- Minimum threshold for new suppliers
- Minimum threshold for existing suppliers

Criteria 4 and 5

Monitoring/audit program

Risk mitigation and capacity building

How are risks addressed to mitigate potential risks?

Expectations:

- Supplier policies/ requirements
- Contract clauses
- Collaborative initiatives
- Audits/corrective action plans
- Capacity building
- Incentives for low-risk behaviours

Risk mitigation and capacity building

How are risks addressed when uncovered within existing suppliers?

Expectations:

- Spend analysis
- Critical supplier analysis
- Risk assessment methodology

Criteria 5

Site visits

Evaluate

How are the efforts working to mitigate risk of slavery?

Expectations:

- Analyse information collected
- Adequacy of measures
- Identify additional improvements can be made/tested
- Refine incentives

Site visits

What does it look like in real life?

Expectations:

- Data gathering
- Check on corrective actions
- Improve engagement
- Performance/KPI measurement

Corrective action plan management/ remediation

How are identified issues remediated?

Expectations:

- Spend analysis
- Critical supplier analysis
- Risk assessment methodology

The key to effectively addressing any risks is to consider who caused or contributed to them. What leverage is available to help remedy problems and mitigate future occurrences? And you must also ensure that the business has allocated responsibility (ownership) and sufficient resources to allow for an appropriate and effective response to cases found.

A TOOL FACTORY IN JINSHAN, ZHEJIANG PROVINCE

This factory applied a recruitment practice often associated with circumventing legal obligations: hiring workers as 'apprentices'.

They would use agents to approach vocational colleges in the interior provinces, and hire a busload of kids, bus them to the factory, and make them work as apprentices. The wage was an apprentice wage, they had little opportunity to get home (because they had been transported several hundred kilometres on a bus hired by the company), and were made to work a normal job.

The factory used this as a means of cheap labour, not providing any particular skills training and not screening for age. This was a clear-cut case of all the indicators being present: deceptive recruiting practices, isolation, vulnerable young workers, and paying less than the legal wage for the work.

From a cultural lens, they couldn't see anything wrong with this approach, and they were not intent on engaging in a full-scale remediation process for all the affected workers, so the only option was to recommend to the client that they cut off this supplier.

SLAVERY INDICATORS

The big question to be asked when talking about indicators for slavery is: can you simply limit the search to slavery?

The answer is a resounding *no*. Slavery exists as an extension to a range of poor employment practices, all of which are not necessarily slavery. Sometimes the line is quite visible, other times it's blurry.

If you go looking for clear-cut cases of slavery you will by extension also be looking for the very visible line. This suggests that you will miss the blurry lines. In my experience, the blurry lines are much more frequent, and the clear-cut cases are few and far apart. In other words, you will miss much if you only look for 'real' cases of slavery.

If, however, you wish to complement your general due diligence and monitoring effort with some pointers leading to slavery, below is an indicators checklist.

Definitions of slavery (including modern day slavery)

Do you know the definition of slavery? Have you ever seen a slave? Few have.

The Commonwealth *Modern Slavery Act 2018* defines slavery as follows:

> The term modern slavery describes situations where coercion, threats or deception are used to exploit victims and undermine their freedom.

Broadly speaking, these situations occur in eight different scenarios, but often they overlap; for example, trafficking is often a result of deceptive recruitment practices.

Slavery scenarios

Trafficking in persons	Slavery
Servitude	Forced labour
Forced marriage	Debt bondage
The worst forms of child labour	Deceptive recruiting for labour or services

Even with these categories, it is a hard task to determine who is and who isn't a slave, unless the person in question speaks up for themselves. Below are some indicators to be used to determine whether someone is a slave or not.

Slavery indicators

Abuse of vulnerability	Retention of identity documents
Deception	Withholding of wages
Restriction of movement	Debt bondage
Isolation	Excessive overtime
Physical and sexual violence	Abusive working and living conditions
Intimidation and threats	

It is important to note that when visiting a supplier site, you will only in the rarest of circumstances be able to pick out who is an actual slave or someone working under slavery-like conditions. Slavery and slave-like conditions exist on a scale, where one end could be seen as just a 'bad or exploitative job' while the other extreme is physically restricting the ability to leave, and being forced into types of work that the person wouldn't otherwise accept.

It's the ability to distinguish the subtle differences which will enable you to identify slavery in the supply chain.

All risk factors play a role, and you will have to understand the external and the internal environment to make an assessment. To understand the internal environment at a supplier's facilities, you can gather observations from a combination of site walk-throughs, staff interviews and reviews of documentation.

Slavery indicators with examples

#	Indicator	Example
1	Abuse of vulnerability	Someone who is vulnerable because they don't speak the local language, and hence cannot communicate and understand local labour rules and regulations.
2	Retention of identity documents	Pakistani workers in UAE having their passports confiscated upon arrival, often using the excuse that they are being held for safekeeping, but they are not returned. This effectively prevents the worker from leaving the employer, or even from returning to his home country.
3	Deception	A friend of the family promises a girl a good job overseas, but it turns out to be gruelling work or even sexual servitude.

#	Indicator	Example
4	Withholding of wages	A Pacific Islander working in Australia being promised that his wages are being paid to his family back home, and the family back home gets told the salary is being paid to their family member overseas working. No one ever sees any money. Because they are geographically separated, there is little chance to discover the deception, and when found out, it may be too late. In China, workers are used to getting paid once a year, when going home for Chinese New Year holidays. In China this is commonly used as a tactic to retain workers during the year.
5	Restriction of movement	A person who is locked up or always under guard; for example, people who are held in labour or political re-education camps in some parts of the world, and made to pay (involuntarily) for their own upkeep by supplying their labour. Could also be prison labour.
6	Debt bondage	A worker taking mandatory 'training', and paying a migration agent a visa fee, plus getting the flight ticket paid for by the agent. The expenses will be charged back to the worker, and if interest is accrued, the salary to pay it back may not cover the repayments. In Hong Kong the Filipino maids often have nothing left for themselves the first three or four months. In the worst of cases, like some places in India and Pakistan, the debt is never paid off, and is passed down for generations.

#	Indicator	Example
7	Isolation	A person who is locked up or always under guard; for example, North Koreans working in Russian timber yards in remote Siberia (also see point 5: Restriction of Movement).
8	Excessive overtime	Excessive overtime is when it goes beyond national law requirements for permissible overtime and/or rest days frequency. It is also excessive if overtime is needed to make minimum wages (when piece rate payment is used).
9	Physical and sexual violence	Some domestic helpers (maids) in Hong Kong, Singapore, Malaysia or Dubai. Often the maid's visa is tied to the employer, making them vulnerable to abuse. Disciplinary measures should never be physical, and they should always be measured rather than excessive.
10	Abusive working and living conditions	Working in facilities without proper PPE and with squalid living conditions. It could be fishing crew on boats in the Andaman Sea. Bunking down below deck or on deck for sleep, no proper equipment and little to no pay.
11	Intimidation and threats	Some domestic helpers (maids) in Hong Kong, Singapore, Malaysia or Dubai. Often the maid's visa is tied to the employer making them vulnerable to abuse. If she wants to leave the employer, but the employer disagrees, it could happen that the employer threaten to have their visa cancelled, leaving them in a critical situation.

Source: ILO indicators of Forced Labour

Indicator

Take notes

Verify finding

Form opinion

When encountering any of these indicators, it's important to note specific details, including time and place, and whether observations can be verified by cross-checking other information sources. You may also extend your inspections beyond the perimeters of the facility to observe free movement of people to and from the facility, the time spent onsite, and other factors. Once starting the process, you can triangulate the information (also referred to as 'weight of evidence') into an opinion or determine the need for more in-depth investigations.

Usually the presence of one indicator is not sufficient to determine if slavery is practised onsite. However, if the indicator is strong enough, it does warrant additional investigations.

Ultimately, the weight of evidence should determine whether slavery is present, and inform the next steps necessary to safeguard your business and its brand through the removal of human rights abuses, including but not limited to slavery.

CHECKLISTS, TEMPLATES AND POLICIES

Templates, checklist and policies disclaimer:

Before reading the section containing templates, checklists and other materials included to assist you in the general process of improving your supply chain and meeting the goals of a sustainable supply chain, a general word on templates and standardised documents is necessary.

The following templates are general in nature and by no means exhaustive. They are intended only as a starting point for the reader.

Anyone deploying templates should take care to ensure that they are fit for purpose, and make amendments to align them to their own business needs and, if need be, acquire relevant external expertise to assist with alignment to their business processes.

POLICIES AND GUIDELINES CHECKLIST

To satisfy the governance criteria in ESG, at the very least you will need to cover the following policies. Whether they are standalone or integrated policies does not matter so much, although maintaining these in an integrated document is a big task.

Ideally, I would recommend having a short and concise reference document with relevant references to the in-depth policies. This makes maintenance easier, because it can be segmented into 'bite-sized' work packages, when policies are reviewed.

You will require at least the following:

- Supplier Code of Conduct

- Human Rights Policy

- Staff Code of Business Conduct

- Procurement Policy

- Ethical Risk Management Policy

- Grievance Policy

- Whistle-blower Policy

- Remediation Policy.

REMEDIATION PLAN

The following remediation plan (often also referred to as the Corrective Action Plan, or CAP) template can be used either by the buyer to keep a record *or* by the supplier to commit to a program of work designed to improve any findings that are in contravention of the buyer's Code of Conduct and/or Standard of Business Conduct documents. Ideally it is used by both entities, to document agreed steps forward.

If the supplier is to develop the remediation plan, it should be submitted no later than 60 days from the finding/audit/visit in case of minor issues and 10 days in the case of major issues (for example, when slavery or child labour is found).

The remediation development process should follow these steps:

1. Analysis, including root cause analysis

2. Solutions

3. Responsibility

4. Resources and budget

5. Implementation strategy

6. Monitoring and follow up

Following is a template which can be used to document the process and the steps taken.

Remediation plan template

For:

Company name:

Supplier ID:

Finding ID:

Day: **Month:**   **Year:**

Audit date to which this remediation plan refers:	Day:		Month:		Year:	

Planned actions:

Action						Responsible
'Step 1'	Day:		Month:		Year:	
'Step 2'	Day:		Month:		Year:	
'Step 3'	Day:		Month:		Year:	
Etc.	Day:		Month:		Year:	

Needs identified:

Policy/Procedure
Documentation/Data management
Communication/Transparency
Training/L&D
Structural change
Stakeholder engagement
Others

Analysis, incuding root cause:

Planned actions:

Person(s) in charge:

'Person 1': 'Step 1'

'Person 2': 'Step 2'

Etc.

Resources needed:

Financial:

Human resources:

Equipment:

Etc.

GRIEVANCE TRACKER

This grievance tracker template can be used either by the buyer to keep a record *or* by the supplier to document actions undertaken to remediate any grievances. Ideally it will be used for both.

A good grievance mechanism addresses four key principles. It should:

1. be legitimate

2. be accessible

3. be transparent

4. facilitate a dialogue.

Grievances can be related to:

*   infrastructure

*   personal relations

*   contractual rights

*   customary rights.

Grievance tracker template

Company name:

Supplier ID:

Grievance identification number:

Date submitted:	Day:		Month:		Year:	

Grievance steps

Hearing of the parties

Yes ☐   No ☐   Comments [_____]

Further investigation needed

Yes ☐   No ☐   Comments [_____]

Conclusion reached and accepted

Yes ☐   No ☐   Comments [_____]

Has a workers' representative been involved?

Yes ☐   No ☐   Comments [_____]

Has the grievance escalated to a higher level?

Yes ☐   No ☐   Comments [_____]

Has the grievance led to a legal case?

Yes ☐   No ☐   Comments [_____]

Using this template helps in gathering and keeping accurate information about any grievance submitted and its investigation, and gives an indication on its resolution. Grievances that have been submitted should be verified by an approved person; that is, an auditor.

A separate sheet for each grievance should be prepared and submitted.

SUPPLY CHAIN MAPPING

Mapping the supply chain is good practice, and it can provide plenty of positive improvements. Mapping it out also assists in addressing the second mandatory criterion in the Modern Slavery Act Guidance.

There is software that can help you gain this oversight, but in the absence of such software, using a template like the following will help buyers and producers map out their supply chain.

Supply chain mapping is generally only performed on significant relationships. In order to determine what 'significant relationships' are, you must define the term first. These significant relationships could be – for example – raw material cotton for a shirt manufacturer or bricks for a construction company.

The purpose of mapping the supply chain is to understand where significant inputs are sourced from, and how they end up becoming the product procured.

An additional benefit is that this is also a useful tool to understand how you, as a business, are able to communicate information up the chain to suppliers beyond the typical line of sight (which often ends at tier 1).

Supply chain mapping template

Business partner company name				
Supplier ID (if any)				
Contact person	First name		Last name	
Email				
Full address	Street and number		Postcode	
	City		Region	
	Province		Country	
Type of business partner (for example, subcontractor, material supplier, recruitment agent, etc.)				
Business partner since (year)				
Number of total workers				
Distance from producer's head office (km)				
Significance of this business partner for the producer (select one)	Low Medium High			
Main season from month to month				
Secondary season from month to month				

Is this business partner part of the internal social management system?	Yes	No
Is it internally audited?	Yes	No
Does it have a social certificate?	Yes	No
Validity date of social certificate (if any)	Day Month Year	
Has it signed our Code of Conduct?	Yes	No
Additional comments about the business partner (if any)		

What is the relationship?

Does this supplier supply other of my suppliers?

Etc.

CHILD LABOUR CHECKLIST

Many of these checklists can seem repetitive in content. This is a result of them being read individually. In real life, the checklists should be integrated across different topics and areas of investigation, and once such integration is achieved repetitive content will be eliminated.

As a standalone checklist, however, it is important not to forget important issues, indicators and red flags as a result of trying to avoid repetition.

Child labour checklist

There are six areas to look into when you begin looking for child labour.

Supplier audit

Do not just jump straight into factory and supplier audits. While audits have their role to play in finding and eliminating child labour, you are better off inspecting a couple of suppliers yourself before engaging a third-party inspection. Jump on an airplane yourself, and make your own assessments to prioritise where to look further and what to do next.

Product

Products from particular industries are known to have a higher prevalence of child labour. If the goods you buy are products where, for example, small hands, good eyesight or low cost as a result of a high-competition environment (which results in wage pressure) is a factor, there is an increased risk.

Country risks

Some countries pose more risk than others. Use the global indices to know which countries pose a higher risk.

Transparency

If you buy from middlemen, such as agents or wholesalers, you may not be able to obtain information about where the product was made at all, which is a red flag. Maybe your tier 1 supplier does not even have this information.

If you buy direct, presumably you have more direct contact with the producer. You may even have visited the factory.

Entity risk

Has the entity been called out before? Can they document what they have done to mitigate other cases? If they cannot document a strong response to a reported case, you may consider what options you have when sourcing that product, and if the supplier is being dishonest or demonstrates real intentions of engaging and improving.

Consequences

As with anything else, there must be consequences. Did you clearly communicate what the consequences for an infraction would be to the supplier? What was the reaction?

You can ask: do you have a policy on child labour? Do you have a CoC? If the supplier does not have a policy on this important issue, how can you expect them to even understand how to comply?

Once all reasonable steps to understand the situation have been taken, trust your gut feeling. If something seems not quite right, probably that gut feeling is right, and you need to apply additional resources to understand the issue at hand first.

SELF-ASSESSMENT QUESTIONNAIRE

The actual formulation of the self-assessment questionnaire (SAQ) is a bit of a science in its own right. It should include:

- general risks

- governance risks

- social risk

- human rights risks

- environmental risk

- stakeholder engagement approach.

This will enable you to get a decent understanding of how your supplier operates and whether you need to move on to performing onsite vetting (also called 'supplier due diligence').

Again, there are several software solutions available enabling risk assessments and filtering of your information according to their algorithms.

The key thing to consider is how this aligns with the general procurement functions SAQ. If certain questions are already answered elsewhere, they should not be duplicated, unless you wish to verify a certain statement. However, verification should not be the goal of an SAQ – that is the purpose of the due diligence.

I would normally avoid questions for which you can deduce the answers; for example, turnover where the turnover will determine if a company is obliged to report according to the *Modern Slavery Act* (or not). If the threshold has been reached, there is no need to ask, 'Are you required to report under the Commonwealth *Modern Slavery Act*?', because clearly the answer is 'yes'. Instead, this question can be replaced with, 'Have you produced a Modern Slavery Statement already?', and provide the option to attach the statement.

The SAQ shouldn't be overly long, as it is a gauge of initial risk, not part of the due diligence process itself.

On the following page are some general examples of the questions you can include in the self-assessment questionnaire, just to get you started. Make sure you include a range of questions that address all of the risks you are examining.

As can be seen, the SAQ questions are (and should be) fairly closed, in that they require an answer either affirming or dissenting. Additional evidence should be provided documenting the claimed status.

This is different to normal interview techniques, which will be used in the audit/due diligence situation, where questions should be of the 'wh-kind': when, where, what, how.

Generic risk

Manufacturing location, raw materials input and subcontractor management

In which countries are the intended production facilities located?	
Are the production facilities wholly or majority controlled by you? (please select 'No' if you will be using subcontractors)	☐ Yes (please provide details) ☐ No (please provide details)

Monitoring

Does your company have a new supplier on-boarding process which include KPIs related to ESG performance?	☐ Yes (please provide details) ☐ No (please provide details)

Governance

Environmental, Social and Governance (ESG) policies and procedures

Does your company publicly disclose its sustainability (or ESG) policies, program, and performance either online or in a sustainability report?	☐ Yes (please provide links) ☐ No (please provide links)

Management systems and standards applied

Does your company use any of the below standards and/or management systems?

☐ ISO 20400 (Sustainable Procurement Guidance Standard)
☐ SA 8000 (Social Accountability)
☐ ISO 26000 (Social Responsibility Guidance Standard)
☐ ISO 14001 (Environment)
☐ ISO 9001 (Quality)
☐ ISO 19600 (Compliance Management System)
☐ ISO 37000 (Anti-bribery)
☐ Etc.

Are the above systems certified?

☐ Yes (provide evidence)   ☐ No

CONCLUSION

Firstly and before summarising and concluding this book, I want to say thank you for taking the time to read it. I hope you have enjoyed reading it as much as I enjoyed writing it.

A POINT OF DIFFERENTIATION

In many ways, the world is getting smaller and the offering consumers have come to expect is getting more streamlined and globally uniform. Consumers in Europe and North America have embraced sustainability, and it is increasingly taken it as a point of differentiation which – importantly – is worth paying extra for.

Investors are also taking note, and seeing not only the consumer demand but also the linkages between ESG, robust governance, business resilience and share value.

Unsurprisingly, European and North American companies have embraced this trend earlier than Australia, and with legal and compliance pressures it's clear that companies that wish to do business in those markets cannot turn a blind eye without leaving money on the table.

Regardless of the market or industry in which you work, if your business wants to successfully compete, crafting an ethical and sustainable supply chain is one of your best differentiators. It won't *continue* being a differentiator, though. As with everything else, eventually consumers will come to expect this standard, but it is not too late to get started.

Don't see a sustainable supply chain as a costly exercise in compliance, but rather see it as an opportunity to invest in the future of your business. At this moment in time in Australia there is still an opportunity to gain a competitive edge which will satisfy customers and consumers as well as staff, investors and other stakeholders.

But don't boil the ocean. Start with what is manageable – but do establish a solid basis for moving forward.

Once defined and once you know what you don't know, get help from someone experienced – someone who has actually seen a real supply chain. This doesn't have to cost a fortune, unless you are after the branding on the report. If you want someone with deep experience, and who provides substance over format, look for one of the smaller boutique expert advisories.

THERE IS A NEED

The content of this book is extracted from my personal experience, and my aim is to share it in an easy-to-read, dip-in dip-out book format similar to my first book. It is my intention to help you bridge the gap between the planning and the communicating, breaking down the problems into an easy-to-understand, step-by-step roadmap, useful for improving and enhancing processes where there is a need.

And there is a need.

I sincerely hope that it has given you some good takeaways that you can easily implement in your business operations for whichever benefit you are pursuing.

Because I believe that there is a lack of experience in this field in Australia, I felt it necessary to share my experience in a way that educates those with less experience, allowing Australian businesses access to qualified and professional services otherwise not easily available in the market.

I approached it from the starting point of understanding why this aspect is important. What drives business and how can this create value?

Then I went through the steps I have been through with countless clients before, trying to demystify the work needed. My hope is that by educating you, the reader, you will have a better understanding of what you can do, what is the minimum, and where you can set stretch targets.

While I tried to create an overall structure, every business is unique and facing its own unique set of circumstances. For this reason there cannot possibly be a ready-made manual for how to manage everything, but hopefully this has been an eye-opener and inspiration, allowing you to get started building your own experience on top of mine, and if you do get started you should have an advantage compared to your competition.

In particular, I hope you have realised how important it is to actually go to the supply chain to see for yourself what is going on. While it's important to have the right policies and processes in any business, at the end of the day the responsibility rests with management – it cannot be fully outsourced. Not actively managing the risks when they can be managed is a potential liability, a liability which can be adequately managed for a relatively modest investment in most cases.

Finally, I hope you have realised that you need to create a plan for the steps you need to take. Often communication is the key to success, so go there, or have someone trusted go there on your behalf.

YOUR OWN SUSTAINABLE SUPPLY CHAIN MONITORING SYSTEM

I wrote this book with the purpose of making it easier for you to set up your own sustainable supply chain monitoring system, which will also allow you to be compliant with the Modern Slavery Act reporting requirements, reduce overwhelm, and ultimately increase the value which can be extracted from these steps, because that's what it's all about: ensuring that your business is built on a solid, profitable and resilient foundation, which will last for years into the future.

By keeping the content of this book in mind, you will have a roadmap full of practical steps which will enable you to do what is expected, without having to experience too many foreseeable pitfalls along the way.

What's next? For support, questions or comments you are most welcome to send an email to Carsten.primdal@gmail.com. You can also join me on LinkedIn (https://www.linkedin.com/in/carsten-primdal/).

On a final note, we must not forget that this is about human beings, in particular those affected by extremely poor working conditions, struggling to put food in the mouths of their children, let alone provide education, healthcare and sanitation. At the end of the day, these are the ones who will reap the biggest benefit from you implementing these policies and processes and tools.

The next step is up to you. I hope you will have more certainty about this complex issue from now on.

ABOUT THE AUTHOR

Carsten is an ESG, Modern Slavery and Sustainable Supply Chain Expert enabling operational transparency by means of developing and implementing practical risk-mitigation processes. While living in China, he remediated several cases of child labour and slavery-like conditions in factories.

Managing a consultancy based out of China (Shenzhen and Hong Kong), servicing business, NGOs, government and the United Nations (ILO) in arranging capacity building projects, worker training, remediation, project impact reviews and ad hoc consultancy projects in China, Bangladesh and Cambodia, he has overseen delivery of capacity-building activities reaching over 2,500 factories and impacting over 125,000 factory workers.

He has delivered projects for a range of clients, including some of the largest retail chains in Australia and Germany (including Woolworths, Lidl, ALDI), as well as for KPMG Australia, Virgin Australia, DB Schenker and others. The projects he has delivered range across ethical business, sustainable supply chain, *Modern Slavery Act* compliance, supply chain security, audit integrity, risk management and compliance.

Having personally consulted onsite to more than 300 factories, he has the practical understanding that can only come from personal experience. It's this practical experience which now enables Carsten to advise businesses on how to improve and how to integrate sustainable supply chain metrics into their ESG frameworks.

Carsten's first book, *Red Flag: Your guide to risk management when buying in China*, is based on his personal experiences living and working in China. *A Roadmap to Modern Slavery Compliance and a Sustainable Supply Chain* outlines the practical steps any business that wishes to improve the sustainability of its supply chain must take to avoid modern slavery and other malpractices. It is also a book based on personal experiences working with sustainable supply chain and ESG issues.

Most of all, and at the core of everything, Carsten is a pragmatist. It's about getting the best result possible considering a range of factors. To deliver his best, he applies his curiosity in conjunction with his skills to create solutions.

You can find further information on his LinkedIn profile: https://www.linkedin.com/in/carsten-primdal/

ALSO BY CARSTEN PRIMDAL

RED FLAG: YOUR GUIDE TO RISK MANAGEMENT WHEN BUYING IN CHINA

Red Flag's foreword by Tue Mantoni (Former CEO, Bang & Olufsen and former CEO, Triumph Motorcycles):

Everyone really wants assurance that what they buy is of the quality and genuine craftsmanship expected, that it is manufactured in circumstances that are acceptable and that it is easy, safe and reliable to operate.

Red Flag's topic is therefore important to almost any business, yet there is not a lot of effort and research going into this area, in particular at smaller companies. For this reason, many businesses unknowingly expose themselves to risks that should be managed proactively. This is in particular relevant when buying and producing in places that are far away from the company's origin or center of gravity.

Having run businesses where quality, design, technological excellence and emotional appeal are critical ingredients, I can say that applying the principles highlighted in this book are very relevant and if applied consistently will help reduce supply chain risk and ultimately help build the reputation of the business and its brand and products.

Providing a deep insight into China and Chinese manufacturing mentality, *Red Flag* is a good starting point for this process. It is written in a clear, down-to-earth style, and along the way it is dotted with the author's own experiences, making it all the more personal.

So don't make the mistake of putting this book aside for later reading. There are not many books on this topic. Read it, understand the principles and get started.

Tue Mantoni
CEO, Bang & Olufsen and previously CEO of Triumph Motorcycles

BIBLIOGRAPHY

The links provided in this bibliography were correct at the time of writing.

AFP & The East African. (2019). 6 NGOs file lawsuit against Total over alleged failure to respect French Duty of Vigilance law in its operations in Uganda. [online] Available at: https://www. business-humanrights.org/en/6-ngos-file-lawsuit-against-total- over-alleged-failure-to-respect-french-duty-of-vigilance-law-in-its- operations-in-uganda?mc_cid=73e1c3f5ae&mc_eid=6b7d929ad1

Anti-Slavery International. (2017). What is child slavery? [online] Available at: https://www.antislavery.org/slavery-today/child-slavery

Cone Communications. (2015). [online] Cone Communications Millennial CSR Study. [online] Available at: https://www.conecomm. com/research-blog/2015-cone-communications-millennial-csr-study

Deloitte. (2018). Millennial Survey 2018. [online]. Available at: https://www2.deloitte.com/global/en/pages/about-deloitte/articles/millennialsurvey.html

Wikipedia. (2019). Capability Maturity Model. [online] Available at: https:// en.wikipedia.org/wiki/Capability_Maturity_Model

Forbes.com. (2017). Two-Thirds Of Corporations Ignore Corruption In Their Supply Chains. [online] Available at: https://www.forbes.com/sites/jwebb/2017/07/19/two-thirdsof-corporations-ignore-corruption-in-their-supply-chains/#4f8df1d7348d

Global Slavery Index. (2018). Australia. [online] Available at: https://www.globalslaveryindex.org/2018/findings/country-studies/australia/

Global Slavery Index. (2018). 2018 Findings: Highlights. [online] Available at: https://www.globalslaveryindex.org/2018/findings/highlights/

Globalreporting.org. (2019). Sustainability Disclosure Database. [online] Available at: https://www.globalreporting.org/services/reporting-tools/Sustainability_Disclosure_Database/Pages/default.aspx

United Nations. (2011). Guiding Principles on Business and Human Rights, Implementing the United Nations 'Protect, Respect and Remedy' Framework. [online] Available at: https://www.ohchr.org/documents/publications/GuidingprinciplesBusinesshr_eN.pdf

The Centre for Policy Development and the Future Business Council. (2016). Climate Change and Directors' Duties (Memorandum of Opinion). [online] Available at: https://cpd.org.au/wp-content/uploads/2016/10/Legal-Opinion-on-Climate-Change-and-Directors-Duties.pdf

Australian Government. (2018). Commonwealth Modern Slavery Act 2018: Guidance for Reporting Entities. [online] Available at: https://www.homeaffairs.gov.au/criminal-justice/files/modern-slavery-reporting-entities.pdf

Human Rights Watch. (2018). Australia: Modern Slavery Bill Falls Short. [online] Available at: https://www.hrw.org/news/2018/07/25/australia-modern-slavery-bill-falls-short

Korruptsioon.ee. (2018). Forms of Corruption. [online] Available at: https://www.korruptsioon.ee/en/what-corruption/forms-corruption

McCrindle. (2015). Australia's Population Map and Generational Profile Update. [online] Available at: https://mccrindle.com.au/insights/blogarchive/australias-population-map-and-generational-profile-update/

Norton Rose Fulbright (2019). Modern Slavery Act: What businesses in Australia need to know. [online] Available at: http://www.nortonrosefulbright.com/knowledge/publications/155473/modern-slavery-act-what-businesses-in-australia-need-to-know/

OECD. (2017). Terrorism, Corruption and the Criminal Exploitation of Natural Resources. [online] Available at: https://www.oecd.org/corruption/Terrorism-Corruption-Criminal-Exploitation-Natural-Resources-2017.pdf

Supply Chain Dive. (2017). The 5 types of supply chain risk. [online] Available at: https://www.supplychaindive.com/news/5-supply-chain-risk-spotlight/448580/

United Nations. (2019). United Nations Global Compact. [online] Available at: https://www.unglobalcompact.org/

United Nations. (2019). How Your Company Can Advance Each of the SDGs. [online] Available at: https://www.unglobalcompact.org/sdgs/17-global-goals

Walk Free. (2016). We can end modern slavery in our lifetime. The Minderoo Foundation. [online] Available at: https://www.walkfreefoundation.org/understand/

www.ingramcontent.com/pod-product-compliance
Lightning Source LLC
Chambersburg PA
CBHW040855210326
41597CB00029B/4860